D0180485

Woman in Mind

December Bee

A play

Alan Ayckbourn

Samuel French – London

New York – Sydney – Toronto – Hollywood

© 1986 BY REDBURN PRODUCTIONS (OVERSEAS) LTD
© 1987. ACTING EDITION, BY REDBURN PRODUCTIONS (OVERSEAS) LTD

1. *This play is fully protected under the Copyright Laws of the British Commonwealth of Nations, the United States of America and all countries of the Berne and Universal Copyright Conventions.*

2. *All rights, including Stage, Motion Picture, Radio, Television, Public Reading and Translation into Foreign Languages, are strictly reserved.*

3. **No part of this publication may lawfully be reproduced in ANY form or by any means—photocopying, typescript, recording (including video-recording), manuscript, electronic, mechanical, or otherwise—or be transmitted or stored in a retrieval system, without prior permission.**

4. Rights of Performance by Amateurs are controlled by SAMUEL FRENCH LTD, 52 FITZROY STREET, LONDON W1P 6JR, and they, or their authorized agents, issue licences to amateurs to give performances of this play on payment of a fee. **It is an infringement of the Copyright to give any performance or public reading of the play before the fee has been paid and the licence issued.**

5. Licences are issued subject to the understanding that it shall be made clear in all advertising matter that the audience will witness an amateur performance; that the names of the authors of the plays shall be included on all announcements and on all programmes; and that the integrity of the author's work will be preserved.

   The Royalty Fee indicated below is subject to contract and subject to variation at the sole discretion of Samuel French Ltd.

   > Basic fee for each and every
   > performance by amateurs   Code M
   > in the British Isles

   In Theatres or Halls seating Six Hundred or more the fee will be subject to negotiation.

   In Territories Overseas the fee quoted above may not apply. A fee will be quoted on application to our local authorized agent, or if there is no such agent, on application to Samuel French Ltd, London.

6. The Professional Rights in this play are controlled by MARGARET RAMSAY LTD, 14A Goodwin's Court, St Martin's Lane, London WC2.

The publication of this play does not imply that it is necessarily available for performance by amateurs or professionals, either in the British Isles or Overseas. Amateurs and professionals considering a production are strongly advised in their own interests to apply to the appropriate agents for consent before starting rehearsals or booking a theatre or hall.

ISBN 0 573 01662 3

WARNING

Publication of this play does not imply it is available for performance. Please do not consider a production before permission is granted. Apply to Samuel French Ltd, 52 Fitzroy St., London W1P 6JR. Performance without permission is an infringement of copyright.

WOMAN IN MIND

Woman in Mind was first performed in Scarborough at the Stephen Joseph Theatre in the Round on 30th May, 1985. The cast was as follows:

Susan	Ursula Jones
Bill	Barry McCarthy
Andy	Robin Herford
Tony	John Hudson
Lucy	Caroline Webster
Gerald	Russell Dixon
Muriel	Heather Stoney
Rick	Tom Bowles

Directed by Alan Ayckbourn
Designed by Adrian P. Smith

Subsequently presented by Michael Codron at the Vaudeville Theatre, London, on 3rd September, 1986, with the following cast:

Susan	Julia McKenzie
Bill	Peter Blythe
Andy	Benedick Blythe
Lucy	Christina Barryk
Tony	John Hudson
Gerald	Martin Jarvis
Muriel	Josephine Tewson
Rick	Daniel Flynn

Directed by Alan Ayckbourn
Designed by Roger Glossop

CHARACTERS

Susan

Bill, her doctor
Gerald, her husband
Muriel, her sister-in-law
Rick, her son

Andy, her husband
Tony, her brother
Lucy, her daughter

The action occurs within forty-eight hours and takes place in Susan's garden and beyond

Time—the present

ACT I

Darkness

We hear the sound of a woman moaning as she regains consciousness. As she opens her eyes, there is bright afternoon garden sunlight. Throughout the play, we will hear what she hears; see what she sees. A subjective viewpoint therefore and one that may at times be somewhat less than accurate. The woman is Susan. She is lying on the grass in the middle of her small, tidy, suburban garden

Susan Aaaah!

Bill Windsor, a pleasant, rather nervous GP is kneeling on the grass a little away from her, attempting to open his medical case without much success. He fails to see her for a minute, so engrossed is he in his abortive task. Susan watches him. She is an unassuming woman in her forties, used to and happy to play second fiddle to more determinedly motivated personalities than her own. Only now, at this stage of her life, is she beginning to question this role she's played or perhaps been cast in. Bill is a year or two younger, eager to reassure, quick to apologize for his own shortcomings. Not though, alas, an instinctive healer of the sick. He notices Susan is awake

Bill Ah! Score ache . . .

Susan (*trying to sit up up*) Waah . . .

Bill Wo! Won't spider slit up pikelet . . .

Susan What?

Bill Skater baby.

Susan (*trying again to sit up, alarmed*) What are you saying . . . ? (*Clasping her head*) Ah!

Bill (*pushing her back, gently*) Squeezy . . . squeezy . . .

Susan Squeezy?

Bill Score grounds appeal cumquat doggy Martha hat sick on the bed . . .

Susan Sick on the what?

Bill Squeezy, cow, squeezy . . .

Susan I've no idea what you're saying. What are you saying?

Bill Saul bite. Saul bite.

Susan Who are you, anyway? Where am I?

Bill Octer bin sir. Climb octer bin sir. Mrs sure pardon choose 'un.

Susan Oh God, I've died. That's what it is. I've died. And—wherever it is I've gone—nobody speaks English . . . What am I going to do? What am I going to do?

Bill Choose 'un, choose 'un. Pea squeak jinglish. Pie squeaking jinglish cow. Choose 'un . . .

Susan (*tearful now*) I'm in hell. I've died and gone to hell.

Bill Choose 'un . . .

Susan Why have I gone to hell? Why me? I've tried so terribly hard, too. Terribly hard ...

Bill Susan ...

Susan You've no idea how hard I've tried. There must be some mistake ...

Bill Susan ... ?

Susan Susan? Yes, that's me. Susan. (*Pointing at herself, loudly, as to a foreigner*) Me Susan, yes.

Bill You're Susan, yes.

Susan Susan, yes. Thank heavens.

Bill December bee?

Susan December bee? Oh, dear God, he's off again. (*Loudly, as before*) No bees in December. Not here. They're asleep. They go to sleep.

Bill Susan, I'm Bill Windsor. Do you not remember me? Doctor Bill Windsor ...

Susan Doctor Windsor? Bill Windsor?

Bill That's it. Well done.

Susan Doctor Windsor, are you dead as well?

Bill (*laughing rather nervously*) No, no. Not as far as I know, anyway. We're both very much alive, Susan. This is your garden. You're in your garden ...

Susan My garden? This isn't my garden ...

Bill Yes, yes, it is. I promise you.

Susan My garden's enormous. Five times the size of this, I can tell you ... (*She tries to rise*) Ah!

Bill No, no. Don't try to sit up, not yet. Easy now, easy. Susan, you've apparently caught a bit of a knock on the head. You're going to feel a bit wobbly for a time so just stay put here ...

Susan Did I bang my head? How did I bang my head?

Bill I think it was the old trick. You stood on the end of the garden rake. Nasty thing to happen.

Susan (*disgusted*) Typical of me. Typical.

Bill I've—er—sent for an ambulance ...

Susan Ambulance? Oh, no, I don't need that.

Bill I'd rather you did if you don't mind. The point is—blows to the head— you never can tell—could be a delayed reaction. Better safe than sorry. Probably just an overnight stop, that's all. Be back home here tomorrow. Right as rain. Probably.

Susan Oh dear, what a nuisance.

Bill There's a little bit of bruising—I had a quick look. Skin's not broken— probably have a nasty lump ... Luckily it won't show much. Under the hair. Still they'll be able to tell at the hospital better than I can ...

Susan They're not going to need to shave my head, are they?

Bill Good Lord, no. You're not going in for brain surgery. At least, I hope not. I'm afraid you'll have to wait for them, if you don't mind. The point is, I'm afraid I'm having a bit of trouble. With my bag there.

Susan Trouble?

Bill Yes, I can't get it open. The lock keeps jamming. I had an accident with it. In my car door. This morning. And. I mean I *can* get it open. In a real emergency. But it does entail a good deal of force in order to do so. And stuff tends to scatter. All over the place. So.

Susan Oh, well. Please don't bother on my account.
Bill Thanks.

A pause. Bill glances at his watch, Susan sits

Well ...
Susan (*sensing his unease*) You don't have to stay if you've——
Bill No, no, no. Best for me to hang on. Just in case—things. Get. (*He looks at his watch again*) Shouldn't be long. (*A sudden thought*) Unless you'd like something. Would you like a glass of water?
Susan No, thank you.
Bill Tea? What about tea? Now, you'd like a cup of tea, wouldn't you?
Susan Well ...
Bill I'll see if I can rustle up a cup of tea. Wait there. I'll do it. I'll also check to make sure she got that ambulance organized. Sit tight. (*He moves away towards the unseen house. Stopping suddenly to listen*) Someone else's not too happy by the sound of it ...
Susan Sorry?
Bill The dog. Next door, is it?
Susan Dog?
Bill Howling. There. Can't you hear it? Hasn't stopped. Probably wants to be let in or—whoops—— (*He trips and nearly falls*)
Susan You all right?
Bill Yes, yes. Always doing that. Accident prone, that's me. You put it there, I'll fall over it. Back in a tick.

Bill exits

Susan sits alone for a moment. It is very quiet with none of the sounds one normally expects to hear in a suburban garden

Susan (*to herself, puzzled*) Dog? I can't hear a dog ...

In the distance, Andy's voice is heard. The garden grows imperceptibly bigger and lighter

Andy (*off*) Susie ... Susie, darling ...
Susan (*calling back*) I'm here, Andy. In the herb garden.

Andy rushes on. A tall, good-looking, athletic man, easy-going and charming. He is perhaps a year or two younger than Susan

Andy Susie? I've just seen Bill Windsor. Are you all right?
Susan I'm perfectly fine, Andy. Just a silly accident, that's all.
Andy (*sitting beside her, immensely concerned*) Darling, what on earth happened? I can't leave you for five minutes, can I? What happened? He said you knocked yourself out ...
Susan I just—banged my head. It's nothing, Andy, really. You mustn't fuss ...
Andy Of course I fuss. You're my wife. I love you. How on earth did you do it?
Susan I'm not even going to bring myself to tell you. Its so ridiculously silly ...
Andy I can't see what you've banged your head on? Unless you stood

on that garden . . . (*Seeing her face*) You didn't stand on the garden rake, darling?

Susan (*mortified*) How could I have been so stupid?

Andy (*fairly amused but doing his best to conceal it*) Oh, you daft thing . . . (*He hugs her*)

Susan (*clinging to him*) It could only happen to someone like me——

Andy We're all going to have to take extra special care of you, aren't we?

Susan —only someone this clumsy could have done it.

Lucy's voice is heard in the distance

Lucy (*off, calling*) Mummy! Daddy!

Andy (*calling*) Over here, chaps. In the herb garden. (*To Susan*) We'll soon nurse you better.

> *Lucy and Tony enter together. Lucy is a tall, good looking, athletic girl, easy-going and charming. She is in her early twenties, and tends to wear fresh, summery, rather timeless dresses. Tony, on the other hand, is a tall, good-looking, athletic man, easy-going and charming. He is aged about thirty. Both appear to be midway through a game of tennis. Tony carries a glass of champagne*

Lucy Is Mother all right? Is she all right?

Andy Don't panic. She'll be OK. She's OK.

Susan Nothing to worry about . . .

Tony What have you been up to now, Big Sis?

Susan Something quite ridiculous, I refuse to tell you. You'll only laugh . . .

Lucy (*indignantly*) We won't laugh.

Susan Yes, you will. I know you two.

Tony (*proffering the glass*) Here, drink this.

Susan What is it?

Tony Champers. I've only just opened it.

Lucy Champagne at eleven in the morning, I ask you. He's actually playing with the glass in his hand.

Tony The thing that's really annoying her is that I'm inflicting a crushing defeat as well. (*Offering Susan the glass*) Here. It is vintage.

Andy Drink it, darling, it'll buck you up.

Susan Do you think I should?

Andy Best possible thing, isn't it, Tony?

Tony Absolutely . . .

Lucy But what happened to Mother? I'm dying to know. How did she bang her head?

Andy Well . . .

Susan Andy, don't you dare tell them. I'm not having them screaming with laughter at me . . .

Lucy We're not going to scream with laughter. Are we, Tony?

Tony Absolutely not.

Susan Well, you might not, Lucy, but he's bound to.

Andy There's no big deal about it. All that happened——

Susan Andy, don't you dare . . .

Andy All that happened was, Susie went into the potting shed and the old tin bath in there slipped off the nail and fell on her——

Lucy Gosh!

Susan Thank you, darling. Thank you.

Tony I loathe and detest tin baths ...

Andy —and she was in such pain she came hopping out of the shed cursing and swearing and stepped on the garden rake ... (*He laughs*)

Susan Andy! You beast!

Lucy and Tony laugh

Tony (*laughing*) Stepped on the rake. I say ...

Lucy (*laughing*) Honestly, Mummy, I didn't know people actually *did* that sort of thing ...

Susan I think you're all absolutely horrid and heartless.

Andy (*taking command*) OK, kids. Joke's a joke. Lucy ...

Lucy Daddy?

Andy We must get your mother upstairs and into bed ...

Susan Oh, Andy, don't fuss——

Andy Ask Mrs Simmonds to make a hot water bottle and light the fire in the master bedroom ...

Lucy Right. (*She turns to go*)

Andy And give her a hand if she needs it. It's Ethel's day off ...

Lucy I'll see to it, Daddy.

Andy Good girl.

Lucy rushes off towards the house

Susan You really do spoil me, all of you ...

Andy Nonsense.

Tony We just want to get you fit so you can carry on slaving for us as usual.

Andy (*taking the empty glass from Susan*) Tony, get your sister another glass of this, will you?

Susan Andy, do you think I should? Bill Windsor's fetching some tea ...

Andy Tea? Oh, to hell with that ...

Tony If it comes to a choice between Dom Perignon or Lapsang Souchong ... Tell you what, I'll bring the ice bucket as well. You can pour it over your head.

Tony lopes off

Susan (*watching him go, affectionately*) He never alters, does he?

Andy Not a tittle. Feel sorry for him in a way.

Susan Sorry? Why?

Andy Well, mostly, when you get a brother and sister like you two, things get shared. She gets the beauty, he gets the brains; or he gets the beauty, she gets the brains. Or even a bit for each of them. But with you and Tony, you've got the lot. All the brains, all the beauty. Hardly fair, is it?

Susan It's not true.

Andy I'm afraid it is.

Susan But I love you for saying it, all the same. (*Starting to rise*) You can leave me now because I'm going to—— (*She sways and nearly falls*) Whoops!

Andy (*catching her and helping her to sit again*) Steady! You are going to do nothing except sit here. As soon as Tony comes back, we're going to carry you up to bed.

Susan (*loving every minute of it*) Oh, Andy . . .

Andy Doctor's orders.

Susan I think Bill Windsor's orders are that I go into hospital for a check-up.

Andy To blazes with that.

Susan He's ordered an ambulance for me.

Andy Bill has?

Susan Apparently.

Andy Oh, Lord. Hang on. (*He moves off*)

Susan Where are you going?

Andy To cancel it.

Susan Cancel it?

Andy I don't want you in hospital, I want you here where we can look after you properly. Get you into that place, we'll never see you again . . .

Susan (*calling him back*) Andy . . .

Andy (*turning back to her*) Hmmm?

Susan Seriously. You do spoil me far too much.

Andy Maybe. I don't know. Perhaps. (*Returning to her*) If we do, I'll tell you why it is. Because we'd all be lost without you. There's only one of you, you see. (*Smiling slightly*) Unfortunately. And we all need you very much. Me most especially. I mean, after all, what does Tony stand to lose? Just a big sister. So what? Plenty of those. Ten a penny. And Lucy? Well—girls and their mothers. We all know what they're like. She'd soon get over it. But me? I'd be losing a wife. And that I'd never get over. Not one as dear and as precious as you. (*He kisses her tenderly*) Whom, incidentally, I love more than words can ever say . . .

Andy moves away, and looking back on her, smiles and leaves, blowing her the gentlest of kisses on one of his fingers

Susan stares after him. The Lights fade upstage. After a slight pause, Susan gives a little strangled moan of pleasure

Bill returns from the direction of the house. As he enters, he speaks to someone who has just passed him who, presumably, could have been Andy

In the distance, briefly, a dog is heard howling to be let in

Bill (*behind him*) . . . right, right, splendid. Did the trick, did it? (*Arriving, to Susan*) Sorry. Small delay. Trying to lend a hand in the kitchen. Fatal. Singed my sleeve. (*He sniffs his jacket*) Ah, well. (*Sniffing the other sleeve*) I spilt liquid paraffin on this one, so it more or less evens it up . . . Feeling any better?

Susan Much better, thank you.

Bill Splendid. It's on its way. I just checked. The ambulance.

Susan Ah. My husband hasn't spoken to you, then?

Bill Your husband?

Susan Yes. He seemed to feel I shouldn't go. He felt I'd be better off staying in bed here.

Bill Really? When did he say this?

Susan Just a minute ago.

Bill Extraordinary. I mean, I didn't even know he was home. I understood he was on his way. He'd been telephoned and was on his way.

Susan Well, he's here. He's just been talking to me.

Bill How odd. Your sister-in-law obviously got it wrong.

Susan My sister-in-law?

Bill Yes—Marion, is it?

Susan You mean my brother?

Bill Muriel. That's it.

Susan Tony.

Bill Tony?

Susan You mean my brother, Tony. Tall, fair, slim, good-looking in a rather weak sort of way . . .

Bill No, definitely Muriel. Short, dark, angular, grim-looking in a rather firm sort of way . . . I haven't seen any Tony at all.

Susan We don't have a Muriel. We have an Ethel but it's her day off. So it can't have been her.

Bill Anyway, the woman in the kitchen. The one who made the tea.

Susan Oh, that'll be Mrs Simmonds.

Bill Mrs Muriel Simmonds?

Susan I've no idea what her first name is, I've never asked her.

Bill But Mrs Simmonds is your sister-in-law?

Susan Certainly not, she's our cook.

Bill Cook?

Susan Yes. She's been with the family for—oh, ages and ages.

Bill (*very puzzled*) Has she? I see (*He pauses*) She—er–seemed to be fairly convinced, in her own mind at least, that she was your sister-in-law.

Susan Did she?

Bill That's the distinct impression she gave.

Susan Well. She can be very strange. (*She pauses*) She's Cornish, I believe.

Bill Is she? One got the overall nuance from talking to her of someone from slightly nearer—South London. Anyway. The woman who found you lying in the garden, the woman who phoned me—or rather phoned your own doctor, Geoff Burgess, who happens to be on holiday, so you got his partner. Me. That woman.

Susan Possibly.

Bill The one who brought you out the tea. That one.

Susan Tea? What tea?

Bill Didn't you get the tea?

Susan Not yet. I thought you were bringing me some.

Bill No. She did. Her. Your Mrs Thing. I passed her just now. She was coming back with an empty cup in her hand.

Susan Really?

Bill So where did the tea go?

Susan Perhaps she drank it herself?

Bill She didn't come out here, then?

Susan I haven't seen her.

Bill No. Yes. I see. (*He stares at her for a moment. He picks up his bag and struggles to open it for a moment. Then, aware that Susan is watching him, he puts it down*)

Susan The only woman that I've seen all day has been my daughter.

Bill Oh, yes . . .

Susan She was playing tennis with Tony.

Bill Tennis?
Susan Yes.
Bill Where?
Susan (*mildly exasperated*) On the tennis court.
Bill Which is—where exactly? From here?
Susan (*with enormous patience*) Over there.
Bill Ah, yes. Silly question.

He looks at his watch. The dog is howling again in the distance

Any minute now. It'll be here.
Susan You know, I don't think you believe me, do you?
Bill Yes, I do. No, no. Yes.
Susan Why don't you believe me?
Bill I do, I do. At least I believe that you believe it. It's just that I personally haven't seen hide nor hair of any of these people.
Susan Well, that's hardly my fault, is it? (*After a slight pause, helpfully*) I can hear the dog now. If that's any help.
Bill Good, good.
Susan You can hear it, too, can't you? (*Anxiously*) You can hear it?
Bill Oh, yes. (*He pauses*) No. I can't. I could but it stopped some time back.
Susan Oh. There's something wrong with me, then, isn't there?
Bill (*cautiously*) I wouldn't say that ...
Susan Well, I suppose there could be with you ...
Bill No, I wouldn't say that either.
Susan What would you say, then?
Bill You—don't recall whether you've got a son by any chance, do you?
Susan A son? Certainly not.
Bill No?
Susan Decidedly not. No, that I would remember. Well, I'd hardly forget whether or not I had a son, would I?
Bill No. It's just—well, I'm not your regular doctor, as I say——
Susan (*impatiently*) I know that. I remember, perfectly.
Bill But I have called on you and your—family in the past. To see your husband. And your—son. On one or two occasions. I think chicken-pox was one. I can't be certain about that.
Susan (*coolly*) You're obviously muddling me up with somebody else.
Bill (*rather significantly*) No, that's not all that likely, believe me.

A pause

These—tennis courts that you can see ...?
Susan I can't see them.
Bill You can't?
Susan No. Can you?
Bill No. That's not the point. The point is, can you?
Susan Of course I can't.
Bill Good. Splendid.
Susan They're round the back of the house.
Bill Oh.

Pause

Susan I can see the swimming pool, if that's any help?

Bill Ah.

Susan And the lawn. And the rose beds and—yes—look, if you stand here on tiptoe you can just see the lake. Look.

Bill (*humouring her, straining to look*) Uh-huh. Uh-huh.

Susan Doesn't it look beautiful today? It's always best in the late afternoon sun.

Bill Yes. yes. (*He consults his watch again*)

A pause

Yes.

Susan (*watching him*) You can't see any of it, can you?

Bill I see—a small garden—very pleasant, very tidy, about twenty feet wide by maybe about thirty foot long . . . There's a little pond over there. Not a lot in it—a stone frog, is it?—I think it's a frog—the thing I fell over, anyway. Some flowerbeds with wallflowers—shrubs, several shrubs—one newly planted. Presumably by you. A rockery there——

Susan Please don't go on.

Bill What?

Susan I don't want to listen to any more of this.

Bill (*gently*) I'm afraid it's what's here.

Susan You're describing some place I wouldn't choose to live in, even in my wildest nightmares.

Bill Oh, I am sorry.

A silence

Susan My brother brought me some champagne, you know.

Bill Did he? Jolly nice.

Susan Dom Perignon. Vintage nineteen seventy-eight.

Bill That's the stuff, eh? (*Laughing awkwardly*) He didn't leave any behind, did he?

Susan (*frostily*) I think it would be better if you went, Doctor.

Bill Oh, I'm not sure that would——

Susan It's all right. I'll arrange an appointment with Doctor Burgess——

Bill He's on holiday——

Susan —as soon as he returns . . .

Bill —for a fortnight. In Spain.

Susan Thank you so much for your help. Good-afternoon.

Bill Look, it's not the afternoon, it's eleven-fifteen in the morning and I really cannot leave you——

Susan I'm only waiting here for my husband, that's all. I'm not going to do anything foolish.

Bill But you will go in the ambulance, won't you?

Susan No.

Bill Ah. Now. I'm sorry. I really must insist you do.

Susan Not unless my husband is agreeable.

Bill Right, fine. Fair enough. We'll hang on for him then, shall we?

Susan If you like. I don't think he will agree. In fact I'm only waiting here because he insists on carrying me up to bed.

Bill Splendid. (*He gathers up his bag*)

Susan wanders away slightly and gazes out

Susan Just look at the rose garden today. A mass of pinks and reds and yellows . . .

Bill stands waiting for a second. Susan continues to stare at her garden

Bill (*hearing something*) Ah, here they come, I do believe.
Susan Good. Now perhaps you'll believe me.
Bill (*to someone off in the distance*) Hallo, good morning. (*Turning to her*) Mrs Gannet? Susan? Remember them now? Your husband and your sister-in-law? (*Gently*) Mrs Gannet . . .
Susan (*turning*) Who on earth's Mrs Gannet when she's——? (*As she speaks and turns, her real family enters. She breaks off. She stares at the two who have just entered*)

First, the Reverend Gerald Gannet, a solemn man in his middle forties. With him his sister, Muriel, much as described by Bill earlier. She is a woman who has known her share of suffering and is anxious others should know about it too. Certainly, as seen through Susan's (and therefore to a large extent our own) eyes, the two present an unattractive picture, entirely lacking the lightness and ease of her earlier family

Gerald Hallo, dear.
Muriel Another cup of tea, Susan?
Susan looks at them in horror. Her knees buckle, she gives a terrible moan and falls into a faint causing a Black-out

During the Black-out, Muriel and Bill exit

There is the briefest of pauses. Then we hear Susan's cry as she jolts awake with a start. The Lights come up abruptly. We are still in the garden. It is morning again. Susan is seated in a garden chair. Another couple of chairs are also in evidence. Gerald is standing nearby. It is he, apparently, who has woken her

Gerald Were you asleep?
Susan (*shaking herself awake*) Yes, I must have—must have dozed off . . .
Gerald It's eleven-thirty. I thought you should know.
Susan Why?
Gerald Rick's here for lunch.
Susan Yes, I know. You told me.

Gerald paces round the garden rather restlessly

Gerald There is a school of thought that believes that sleep is for the night. You seem to be out to disprove them . . . Is that bush dead? It looks dead from here.
Susan I'd sleep at night if I could. I'm finding it very difficult recently . . .
Gerald Hardly surprising. If you sleep all day.
Susan (*rather irritably*) What do you want, Gerald? Do you want me to do something for you?
Gerald No, no. Don't stir yourself on my account. I was just taking a brief break from the book. Thought I'd see what you were doing. Now I know. Sleeping.

Susan Might I remind you, I only came out of hospital this morning.

Gerald Presumably they released you because they considered you fit and well. Anyway, Bill Windsor just phoned. Said he'd look in later.

Susan Oh, he doesn't have to bother ...

Gerald Ask him for a tablet or something. To help you sleep. At night. Or perhaps a stimulant. To keep you awake. In the daytime.

Susan Has it ever occurred to you why I can't sleep at nights?

Gerald Insomnia?

Susan Perhaps it's because I'm not very happy, Gerald.

Gerald Well, who is? These days. Very few.

Susan You seem happy.

Gerald Do I? Maybe I'm just better at hiding these things. Who knows?

Susan At least you sleep at night.

Gerald Only because I'm exhausted from a full day's work. I give my body no option.

Susan Zonk.

Gerald I beg your pardon?

Susan You just zonk out.

Gerald I've no idea what that means. Zonk? There's your solution. Fill your day a bit more. Then you'll sleep.

Susan (*flaring*) I work extremely hard, Gerald, and you know it. I help you whenever I'm able. I run this house for you——

Gerald With the help of my sister, you do——

Susan No, Gerald, *despite* Muriel's help, I run this house. I do all the cooking, the bulk of the washing up, *all* the laundry—including Muriel's—I cope with the sheer boring slog of tidying up after both of you, day after day, I make the beds, I——

Gerald All right. All right, dear. We don't need the catalogue. All I am saying is—you still don't seem to have enough to do.

Susan No, you're absolutely right, Gerald. I don't. Not nearly enough. Not any more.

Gerald Something the matter?

Susan There must be. I don't know what my role is these days. I don't any longer know what I'm supposed to be doing. I used to be a wife. I used to be a mother. And I loved it. People said, "Oh, don't you long to get out and do a proper job?" And I'd say, "No thanks, this is a proper job, thank you. Mind your own business." But now it isn't any more. The thrill has gone.

Gerald Oh, we're back on that, are we?

Susan 'Fraid so ...

Gerald "The trivial round, the common task, Will furnish all we need to ask ..."

Susan Yes, it's usually about now that you come up with that invaluable piece of advice, Gerald. The point is it's not true. They don't. Furnish. All we need to ask. Not on their own. Whoever wrote it was talking through his hat. Anyway, how can you possibly believe anybody who rhymes "road" with "God" ...

Gerald All one can say is that they're words that have provided comfort to several generations ...

Susan Good-o.

Gerald (*suddenly irritated by her*) If you want something to do, why don't you pull up that dead bush?

Susan It's not dead. I planted it yesterday. In between hitting myself on the head ...

Gerald How is the head?

Susan Fine. The bump's going down. Scarcely feel it.

A silence. Gerald walks about again

Gerald Bill Windsor was telling me you'd been – hallucinating.

Susan Was he?

Gerald Apparently you saw people. Is that so?

Susan I thought doctors were supposed to treat things in confidence ...

Gerald He told me. I'm your husband. He felt I should know. In case it happened again. Has it happened again?

Susan No.

Gerald (*amused by this*) What sort of people did you see? Were they nice? I hope so.

Susan Very nice, thank you. Most attractive and dishy.

Gerald It was a—sexual—thing, then, was it?

Susan No.

Gerald No?

Susan Not really.

Gerald Was—was I there?

Susan No, you were not. Nobody I knew was there. Except for Bill Windsor, of course ...

Gerald Bill Windsor? Good Lord, do you mean you were fantasizing over Bill Windsor?

Susan No. Bill was just there.

Gerald What was he doing?

Susan Nothing much. Struggling with his bag. Falling over frogs ...

Gerald Much the same as he does in real life.

Susan It was real life.

Gerald I thought you said this was a fantasy?

Susan It was. Bill was real. The rest was a fantasy. Oh, I can't explain it. You wouldn't understand, anyway.

Gerald I don't know. Some would say, that for a man in my line of business, it was very much up his street. (*He laughs at this*) I mean as a specialist in matters unseen ...

Susan Yes, all right, Gerald. That's a jolly good joke ...

Gerald But I can't be of help in your case?

Susan We've known each other rather a long time, haven't we?

Gerald Said by anybody else, that could have been interpreted as quite an affectionate remark. Spoken by you, it sounds like an appalling accusation.

Susan (*offhandedly*) Well, you know I don't love you any more, Gerald. You knew that.

Gerald Yes. I did know. (*He pauses*) I don't think you've ever said it—quite so baldly as that before—but I got the message ...

Susan I'm still reasonably fond of you.

Gerald Yes?

Susan Most of the time. Well, don't look so glum. You don't love me, either.

Gerald Yes, I do.

Susan Oh. Come on ...

Gerald I do. At least, I'm not aware that my feelings towards you have altered that much——

Susan What? Not at all?

Gerald Not that I'm aware of——

Susan Oh, Gerald——

Gerald I still feel the same——

Susan We don't kiss—we hardly touch each other—we don't make love—we don't even share the same bed now. We sleep at different ends of the room——

Gerald That's just sex you're talking about. That's just the sexual side——

Susan Well, of course it is——

Gerald There's more to it than that, surely?

Susan Not at the moment there isn't.

Gerald You mean that the—sex—is the only thing that's mattered to you in our relationship?

Susan Of course not.

Gerald That's what you seem to be saying.

Susan What I'm saying is ... All I'm saying is, that once that's gone—all *that*—it becomes important. Over-important, really. I mean before, when we—it was just something else we did together. Like gardening. Only now I have to do that on my own as well. It was something we shared. A couple of times a week. Or whatever——

Gerald More than that. More than that.

Susan Yes. Whatever. The point is that then, everything else, the everyday bits, just ticked along nicely. But take that away, the really joyous part of us—and everything else rather loses its purpose. That's all.

A pause

Gerald What you're really saying is, that I've let you down. Failed to deliver. Is that it?

Susan That's not what I mean. It's nobody's fault. It just happened, over the years.

Gerald My fault. I see.

Susan I knew you'd say that.

Gerald That's how you make it sound, anyway. (*He paces about*) I rather thought you'd lost interest in all that, you know.

She does not answer

I thought that when a woman got to—our age—she more or less ... switched off.

Susan Yes, well, I'm a freak, Gerald. I'm afraid you married a freak ...

Muriel comes from the house at this moment bearing a tray with some dubious-looking cups of coffee

Muriel I thought I'd make some coffee. Since nobody else was ...

Gerald (*now full of bonhomie*) Ah, bless you, Muriel.

Susan has closed her eyes

Muriel's made us a nice cup of coffee, dear.

Susan Goody, goody, goody . . .

Muriel I hope it's all right. Susan generally manages to find something wrong with my coffee . . . I'd have thought she'd have made some herself by now, rather than leaving it to me . . .

Susan ignores them

Gerald (*in a loud whisper*) She's in a little tiny bit of a mood, Muriel. Don't worry.

Muriel (*whispering in turn*) Oh. Do you want me to go?

Gerald Heavens, no. Stay here. Sit here with us. You can help cheer things up.

Susan makes a mirthless, laughing sound. Muriel sits down with them

Muriel This garden could do with a tidy, couldn't it? That bush is dead.

Susan (*eyes closed*) You're welcome to take over any time, Muriel.

Muriel I wouldn't dare. Not after last time. I learnt my lesson. She went on and on at me . . .

Susan Because you stuck a garden fork through the bottom of the pond——

Muriel I did no such thing——

Susan You murdered my goldfish, Muriel. I shall never forgive you.

Gerald This is an interesting cup of coffee, Muriel.

Muriel Nice?

Gerald Very interesting. Yes.

Susan (*examining her cup for the first time*) What powder did you use?

Muriel Here we go, the Spanish Inquisition——

Susan I was only curious——

Muriel I used the coffee in the tin marked "Coffee". All right?

Gerald That sounds logical to me . . .

Susan Yes, it is. Fairly. This is the ready-ground coffee, Muriel, not instant . . .

Muriel I don't know what sort it is. If you don't want it, I'll take it back . . .

Gerald No, no, this is perfect, Muriel. First rate.

Muriel (*muttering*) Can't do anything right, can I?

Susan Delicious, Muriel. You must give me the secret.

Gerald Susan, now . . .

Muriel (*muttering*) I don't know what she's talking about, I'm sure. You just put it in a cup and pour water over it, don't you?

Gerald Perfect. (*He smiles at Muriel*)

Pause

Muriel I don't know why I'm suddenly this terrible cook. Why I'm suddenly made to feel so incompetent. I nursed our mother perfectly satisfactorily for her last twelve years . . .

Gerald True, true . . . You gave away your prime, Muriel.

Muriel I did. And my dear, late, bedridden husband Harry for another seven. I cooked three meals a day, seven days a week, three hundred and sixty-five days a year for that man until the day he died . . .

Gerald (*murmuring*) Yes. Amazing. Amazing.

Muriel So. I didn't do so badly.

Susan I've no doubt you'll see us all off as well, Muriel.

Muriel (*indignantly*) Well ...

Gerald That's a very unfeeling remark, Susan ...

Susan Sorry.

Gerald In view of Muriel's past and present sufferings and tribulations, I think the least you can do is make allowances ...

Susan Sorry, sorry, sorry ...

Muriel Got out of bed the wrong side this morning, didn't she?

Susan Fat chance of that. It's over the other side of the room.

Gerald Now, now, now ...

Pause

Muriel I didn't sleep again.

Gerald (*sympathetically*) No?

Muriel I felt him very close again last night ...

Gerald Harry, this is?

Muriel At one point, I sensed him—even though my eyes were closed—bending over me, gazing into my face. I felt his breath on my cheek. And the room went deathly cold. Do you think it's possible, Gerald, that he's trying to get back to me?

Gerald Well frankly, Muriel, I have to be honest. I don't hold out all that hope. I have to say that——

Muriel But he's still there, Gerald ...

Gerald Oh, yes, I'm sure he's there, Muriel. I'm certain he's there. Somewhere. It's just really the nature of where is *there*. You see I don't think that *there* is necessarily *here*. If you follow.

Muriel No ...

Susan Extremely unlikely, I'd have thought.

Muriel (*coolly*) I don't know what you know about these things, Susan.

Susan Nothing at all. But it does seem to me that God, in his infinite wisdom and with the entire cosmos to choose from is unlikely to base the Kingdom of Heaven around Muriel's bedroom.

Gerald That is not only facetious, Susan, that is also blasphemous.

Susan I'm sorry, Gerald.

Gerald I hardly think that it's me you should be apologizing to.

Susan Sorry, God.

Gerald I actually meant to Muriel.

Susan Oh, rather. Let's get our priorities right. Muriel, then God, then Gerald. I've got it. Sorry, Muriel.

Gerald opens his mouth to speak, then thinks better of it. A silence

Gerald (*not moving*) Well, I think I must ... Back to the book.

Muriel My dear friend Enid Armitage—when she lost her fiancé in the rail crash of nineteen fifty-nine ...

Gerald I remember. I remember your friend Enid ...

Muriel She willed her Desmond back to her. She willed him back. Every night, before she went to sleep, every night for three and a half years she concentrated on Desmond's image, willing him back. Not that she ever saw him. But one morning she woke up, she opened her eyes and there, on the bedroom ceiling, written in this dark sort of chalky substance: "LOVE ... ENID ... ETERNALLY ..."

Gerald Yes, I do remember it. It caused quite a sensation.

Muriel Written there in a chalky substance. Over her head when she woke.

Gerald Yes. (*He pauses*) I recall, though, that they did establish it was Enid's handwriting, didn't they?

Muriel Oh, yes. But then he worked through her hand, didn't he? Desmond made use of her hand ...

Susan (*murmuring*) I hope he put it back when he'd finished with it ...

Muriel (*ignoring this*) And remember this. They never did find that chalk, did they?

Gerald Perfectly true.

Muriel (*half to herself*) "LOVE ... ENID ... ETERNALLY ..."

Gerald You going to sleep again, Susan?

Susan Not quite ...

Gerald Well, don't forget Rick's here for lunch, will you?

Susan So you keep saying.

Muriel We didn't get a lot of notice, did we?

Gerald Oh, you know what Rick's like. I only got his letter this morning ...

Muriel We should be getting things ready, shouldn't we? If Rick's coming. I mean I'd do it but I don't like to do it.

Susan Don't bother. He won't want anything to eat. Just a few nuts and berries from the hedgerow ...

Gerald He'll need something. He's coming from Hemel Hempstead.

Susan I'll put him out a glass of rainwater, then.

Gerald Your usual motherly self, I see.

Susan Well, he's hardly particularly filial, is he? We haven't seen him for two years ...

Gerald (*wearily*) You know why that is. This particular philosophical group——

Susan Now he won't even speak to us ...

Gerald That's just one of their rules, that's all. Heavens, theirs isn't the first example of a silent order. Think of the Cistercians ...

Susan They were slightly less discriminating. I mean, correct me if I'm wrong, but Trappists aren't just forbidden to talk to their parents, are they?

Muriel I don't know what you know about these things, Susan, I'm sure.

Gerald He still writes letters, doesn't he? Very newsworthy letters ...

Susan He does. To you.

Gerald That's the way they are. The boys write to their fathers, the girls write to their mothers ...

Susan Girls? You mean they've got girls joining now?

Gerald One or two, I believe.

Susan (*laughing*) That'll terrify the life out of Ricky.

Gerald Nonsense.

Susan The only reason he joined, so far as I can make out, was to avoid meeting women.

Gerald Don't be so ridiculous ...

Susan They frighten the life out of him.

Gerald (*stung by this slur on his son*) If they do, I think we can easily see the cause.
Susan Me?
Gerald Oh, yes . . .
Susan I hardly ever saw the boy. You bullied him into that scholarship and then packed him off to that piddling little public school where he never saw anything female aged under fifty-five or weighing less than fifteen stone till the day he left . . .
Gerald Let's not get into this, Susan.
Susan You forget I used to have to listen to his prayers every night of his holidays, Gerald. "Please God, don't make me have to get married."
Gerald That is nonsense . . .
Susan That's what he used to say . . .
Muriel I don't know what you know about these things, Susan . . .
Susan Poor little sod. Sixteen years old and, until I told him, he thought his bed got damp in the night because the roof leaked. You did nothing for him, Gerald. Nothing. He could have died for all you cared. And now he's grown up he won't even speak to me—— (*She breaks off, suddenly very tearful*)

A silence. The dog starts howling in the distance

Muriel (*starting to gather up the cups*) If we've all finished, I'll . . . clear these up . . .
Gerald Yes. I must get on. Do another half-hour on the book.
Muriel Shall I bring you another cup, Gerald?
Gerald (*rather hastily*) No, Muriel, no, thank you. Don't want to spoil my lunch.
Muriel Hark at that poor little dog, isn't it terrible? Why doesn't she let him in when he howls like that?
Gerald I think old Mrs Ogle's just a little bit deaf, Muriel, that's the problem . . .
Muriel Well, she ought to do something about it, oughtn't she?
Susan (*savagely*) Like shoot it . . .

Muriel tuts at this and goes off with the cups towards the house

Gerald hovers awkwardly, feeling something more need be said

Gerald He always sends his love, you know. Rick. When he writes. He always sends you his love.
Susan Does he? You must send mine back then, mustn't you?
Gerald Yes, I usually do. When I write. Well.

At this point, Lucy, now in a light, flowing summer dress comes chasing past them laughing. The sound is very faint. Tony comes on in pursuit. They chase off

Susan watches them. Gerald looks at Susan, puzzled

What is it?
Susan Nothing.
Gerald You looked as though you'd seen something?
Susan Only a bee.

Gerald A bee?

Susan A December bee.

Gerald (*seeing someone approaching*) Ah, here he is. Bill Windsor's arrived. (*Calling*) Morning, Bill!

Bill arrives, tripping as he comes

Bill Hallo, there—whoops——

Gerald (*laughing*) Careful, Bill, careful . . .

Bill (*looking at what he tripped over*) That's my friend the frog again, I think. Is it a frog?

Susan It was.

Bill And how are things here . . . ? Good-morning, Susan.

Susan Hallo.

Bill How are you today?

Gerald Well, the bump's gone you'll be glad to hear . . .

Bill Has it? Good, good. I hoped it would. Any more hallucinations?

Gerald Apparently not.

Bill Splendid.

Gerald No more visitations.

Bill Ah, that's healthy. How's she sleeping?

Gerald Well, that's a bit more of a problem. She's not getting her sleep at nights, at all . . .

Bill Oh, dear . . .

Gerald So she's tending to drop off during the day. Which isn't the way, of course . . .

Bill No, no. I think I might prescribe her a mild sedative then, Gerald. She's not allergic to that sort of thing, is she?

Gerald No, no . . . I don't think so.

Bill Right. (*Leaning in to Susan, confidentially*) Everything else working normally, is it? Waterworks? Other bits?

Susan I've no idea. You'd better ask my husband.

Bill (*puzzled*) Sorry?

Susan (*moving away from them*) I'm fine now, Bill, absolutely fine . . .

Gerald Don't forget Rick's here for lunch, will you, dear?

Susan (*with a flashing smile*) Oh, heavens above! Thank you for reminding me, I practically forgot.

Bill Rick? That's your son, Rick? (*He looks at Susan for confirmation*)

Susan Yes. I remember him now. It's all right.

Bill Good, good. You keeping busy, Gerald?

Susan moves away from the men and wanders a little as they talk, half listening to them

Gerald Well . . . just finishing off the book, you know.

Bill Really? Are you on a book? Bursting into print, are you? Clever chap.

Gerald (*modestly*) Well, it's a small little venture. Nothing earth-shattering. I was commissioned by the Civic Society—it's a short history of the parish. For the centenary, you know.

Bill Oh, you mean next year's shindig?

Gerald That's the one. Just a few thousand words, you know. Trying to condense six hundred years into sixty pages . . .

Bill Well, I take my hat off to you. I doubt I even know a few thousand words. Let alone start writing them down. Unless you're allowed to repeat some?

They laugh and move further away from Susan

Gerald (*his voice fading away as they move out of earshot*) I'll tell you what I've been wanting to ask you, Bill. It's whether . . .

As Gerald is speaking, Lucy enters and comes to Susan carrying two glasses of champagne

The men, naturally, are unaware of her and continue a silent conversation of their own

Lucy Mummy, Daddy says lunch will be ready in fifteen minutes and you're to drink this because you still look far too pale and interesting . . .
Susan Oh, Lucy, I'll be legless if I do . . .
Lucy Good. I'll join you. (*Raising her glass*) Here's to the family!
Susan (*responding*) The family!

They drink

Is Daddy coping in the kitchen?
Lucy Of course he is. He's being his ace super chef. Everybody stand back. He's making that wonderful salmon dish with his own special mayonnaise. And I think he's made summer pudding and some homemade peach sorbet—Oh, just mountains and mountains as usual. Enough for an army . . .
Susan He never learns . . .
Lucy And Tony and I have volunteered to tidy up after him—which should take us the rest of the afternoon. Meanwhile you are allowed just to lounge around here getting as legless as you like.
Susan No, that's not good enough, I've got work to do as well, you know . . .
Lucy On your book? Super. How's it coming?
Susan (*with a quiet confidence*) All right, I think. I've done all the slog, all the heavy research, now I can actually get down to real writing . . .
Lucy I think you're amazing. I don't know how you do it.
Susan (*shrugging*) Well . . .
Lucy We're just all so proud of you, Mummy, you've no idea. I know you won't read these things, but did you know that last Sunday in the *Observer*, they called you probably our most important living historical novelist . . .
Susan Did they, darling? Well . . . it was the *Observer*—The point is, darling, I don't think that any writer can take——

She breaks off as Gerald hails her from a distance

Gerald Dearest, Bill says he'll stop for lunch. All right?
Susan Fine.
Gerald We'll have enough, won't we?
Susan Mountains.
Bill Thank you . . .
Susan (*softly*) Salmon and summer pudding and sorbet . . .

Bill Sorry?

Susan It'll only be frozen quiche, I'm afraid.

Bill Oh, first class. We live on them.

Gerald You all right, darling?

Susan Yes.

Gerald What were you doing?

Susan Trying to remember a poem . . .

Gerald It's twenty to one . . . Don't forget——? No.

Gerald and Bill resume their tête-à-tête. They are evidently now talking about Susan. Shortly, under the next, unnoticed by Susan, they both go off to the house

Susan returns her attention to Lucy who has been sitting, throughout the last, deep in thought

Lucy Mummy, now I've got you on my own, there's something I desperately want to tell you . . .

Susan What's that, darling?

Lucy It's just that I've met someone I love very much and we want to get married.

Susan (*touched*) Oh, darling.

Lucy Are you upset?

Susan Upset? Why should I be upset?

Lucy You're crying . . .

Susan That's only—That's only because I'm so happy for you . . .

Lucy (*hugging her*) Oh, Mummy. (*Now very excited and bubbling*) He's amazing. You'll love him, too. I know you will. He's witty and charming and handsome and tender——

Susan I know, I know he will be——

Lucy You know? How?

Susan Oh, I just know. When can I meet him?

Lucy Soon. May I invite him round?

Susan Of course . . .

Lucy I hope Daddy likes him——

Susan He will.

Lucy And Tony. I want you all to like him.

Susan They will. We'll make sure they do. You and me.

Lucy Yes. That's why I told you first. And I always will. I'll tell you everything first. I promise.

Susan Thank you, darling . . .

Lucy Now. More champers?

Susan looks doubtful

You must. To drink my health.

Susan All right. Just one more.

Lucy (*scrambling away*) I'll be back soon . . .

Lucy goes, taking Susan's glass

Susan watches her

Susan (*with a sudden thought*) Oh, Lord. Lunch. What am I doing?

Susan makes to leave, passing Bill, as he returns

Bill Hallo. Where are you off to?

Susan Do excuse me, I should have started lunch. Sorry, I got carried away with something else.

Bill Hey, well, no, wait. It's all right. It's all under control.

Susan (*stopping*) Is it?

Bill I've just been telling Gerald that, in my view, you're still not a hundred per cent. You've got to take it easier, you know.

Susan No, I'm better, really.

Bill One more day taking things quietly. That's all. Promise. Won't do you any harm. For me.

Susan Well. We won't get any lunch.

Bill Your sister-in-law was delighted to take over.

Susan Was she? I bet.

Bill She's going to fix us all a light snack.

Susan Light?

Bill Omelettes, apparently.

Susan Oh, yes, I remember them. There is—this frozen quiche if you'd prefer it.

Bill No. An omelette aux fines herbes sounds rather delicious.

Susan Yes, doesn't it sound it . . .

Bill Hope you don't mind me gatecrashing. I'm afraid I more or less invited myself. I didn't intend to. Nora, my wife, she's away at the moment, you see. Having a well-earned holiday. In Portugal. So I'm afraid I'm scrounging meals where I can.

Susan You may live to regret it. At least, I hope you will. Live, I mean.

Bill laughs

Lucy enters during the next with a glass of champagne

Bill Gerald was telling me that—Shall we sit down?

Susan Yes, of course.

Bill adjusts the chairs. Susan notices Lucy

(*To Lucy*) Just put it there, darling, thank you.

Lucy Right.

Bill Right you are.

Lucy goes

(*Plonking the chair down as instructed*) That all right for you there?

Susan Thank you. (*Sitting*) Did I—? Did I say something just then?

Bill When?

Susan While you were moving the chairs?

Bill Er—yes. You said—just put it there. Darling.

Susan I did?

Bill Did you—not know you'd said it?

Susan Yes, I knew I'd said it. I was just checking if you'd heard it. You had.

Bill Yes. I had. (*He smiles at her*)

Pause

No more hallucinations, I hope?

Susan No. No. (*After a slight pause*) No.

Bill Sure?

Susan Positive.

Bill These things can linger on, you see. Sometimes. Do you get much of a chance to relax at all? Any hobbies, that sort of thing?

Susan Not really. I watch far too much television, if you call that relaxing.

Bill Oh, yes. Rather. Best sleeping draught there is.

Susan The problem is I watch such trash most of the time, I just sit there feeling guilty. Saying to myself, what on earth am I doing watching *this*? Why aren't I watching something useful? I mean, I do try sometimes to watch interesting programmes but I find them all so boring. I read a bit.

Bill Good, good.

Susan Not the right books, of course. Historical romances, that sort of thing.

Bill Ah.

Susan I can see you thoroughly disapprove.

Bill Not at all. What's a *right* book, for heaven's sake? I read science fiction.

Susan Do you?

Bill All the time.

Susan Well. I don't feel so bad then.

Bill Do you play any sports?

Susan Good Lord, no.

Bill Not a bad idea. To take up something. It doesn't have to be squash.

Susan I—I did think about riding. Learning to ride. But I think it's a bit late at my age. Sitting astride some aged, minute pony with hundreds of giggling seven-year-olds looking on. I desperately wanted a horse when I was young but . . .

Bill Couldn't you?

Susan No, my father didn't approve.

Bill Of horses?

Susan Of animals. Dogs, cats, hamsters, horses. He had a theory that they gave off diseases . . .

Bill Well, he was right, they do. They also give off an awful lot of happiness. Which probably balances it up in the long run. People may catch diseases but at least they die happier. So no horse?

Susan No. No pets at all.

Bill Shame.

The conversation seems to have lowered Susan's spirits somewhat

(*Changing the subject*) Your husband was telling me about his book. Sounds a cracker.

Susan What, his history of the parish since thirteen eighty-six? Yes.

Bill Going to be very interesting, I'd have thought.

Susan Oh, yes.

Bill Fascinating.

Susan But only to people who've lived here.

Bill Oh, yes.

Susan Preferably since thirteen eighty-six.

Bill What? Oh. (*He laughs*) Lot of hard work.

Susan Oh, yes. (*She pauses*) Actually, Gerald's been working on it since thirteen eighty-six.

Bill laughs a lot at this one

Bill Thirteen eighty-six ... yes. (*He pauses*) Your son's due shortly.
Susan Yes.
Bill He's your one-and-only, isn't he?
Susan Yes. Our one-and-only. We'd probably have had more if it hadn't been for my husband's book ...
Bill Oh, yes?
Susan That's tended to burn up most of his midnight oils. If you follow me.
Bill (*philosophically*) Ah, well. I know how these things can get you. Hobbies and so on. I'm—er—I'm actually into macramé, would you believe? You know, the old knotted string bit.
Susan Really? I'd never have thought of you doing that. How clever.
Bill I'm still at rather early stages, I'm afraid. I spend most of the night unpicking it. But Nora's all for it. Well, she introduced me to it. Very encouraging. She's even let me have the spare bedroom.

Gerald enters. In one hand, he has a tray with a dusty bottle of sherry and some assorted glasses. In his other hand, a small folding card table

Gerald The sum total of our drink supply appears to be a bottle of Marsala. I don't know if anyone cares for Marsala.
Bill Marsala. Well, that sounds like a challenge. Why not?
Gerald (*struggling*) Thank you, Bill. If you could—— (*He indicates for Bill to take the tray from him*)
Bill (*doing so*) Oh, righto.
Gerald Thank you.

Gerald puts up the card table whilst Bill holds the tray

Splendid. Now can we put that on here like so. (*Putting the tray on the table*) And I hereby declare the bar open. (*Looking enquiringly at Susan*) Dearest ... ?
Susan What I'd love more than anything else is a glass of Marsala.
Gerald It's your lucky day. (*He laughs*) Bill?
Bill (*joining in the joke*) Er—I suppose you've got nothing in the house at all like—Marsala, have you? No?
Gerald No. Sorry. We've got Marsala if that's any good?
Bill Marsala? No, not heard of it. Never mind, I'll try that.

Both men laugh

Susan (*under her breath*) Oh, my God. What did I start?
Gerald (*never one to let a good joke go*) And I think ... (*Deliberating*) Well, yes, I'll have the same. Why be different?
Bill Why indeed?
Gerald Good health, then.
Bill Good health.
Susan Cheers!

They drink. Susan and Bill react variously. Gerald seems happy with his drink

Bill When did you last see your son, then?

Gerald Who, Rick? Oh, must be two years.

Bill Been away?

Gerald Yes.

Bill Abroad?

Gerald No, no. Hemel Hempstead.

Bill Ah. Working there, is he?

Gerald No. He's—he's studying.

Bill Right. What does he find to study in Hemel Hempstead, then?

Gerald Er . . .

Susan He belongs to this sect.

Gerald No, it's not a sect, dear. It's a group. They prefer you to call them a group.

Bill A religious order?

Gerald Mmm. Mmm. Yes. Not I think strictly what one would term religious. Not in the conventional sense. Philosophical, perhaps, is nearer the mark.

Susan Cranky.

Gerald Now, now, Susan. We've agreed we mustn't prejudge.

Susan I didn't and I have.

A slight pause

Bill You'll be—looking forward to seeing him, no doubt.

Gerald Oh, yes. (*At his drink*) I think this is rather pleasant. It may be a bit sweet for you, dear, is it?

Susan It's lovely. (*She drains her glass and puts it down*)

Bill If you want to chat to him, catch up on all his news, please don't worry about me. I'll be happy to sit and listen.

Susan I think I got that stuff for cooking. Years ago.

Gerald Ah.

Bill He'll probably want to chatter on, won't he? My two do. Whenever they're home. Can't get a word in.

Gerald Really? Well. It takes all sorts.

Susan The point is, Bill, our son doesn't talk to us at all.

Bill No?

Gerald Susan . . .

Susan Bill has to know, Gerald, if he's staying for lunch. Otherwise he'll wonder what on earth's going on. All of us miming to each other over the table.

Gerald I don't feel we necessarily need to share our little family problems with everyone . . .

Susan Little?

Bill Should I go? Would you rather I went?

Gerald (*sharply*) No!

Susan (*sharply*) No!

Gerald Please. Stay. It would, actually, be easier if you did, Bill. For us. So please. It's a phase we're both praying he'll grow out of—it's all to do with this group's somewhat over-emphatic reading of Matthew Chapter Ten, I suspect. Verses thirty-six and thirty-seven—" . . . and a man's foes shall be they of his own household . . ." et cetera. Or again, Mark Chapter

Three verses thirty-one to thirty-five——
Susan Yes, I think Bill's got the idea, Gerald ...
Bill So he won't be speaking to you? At all?
Gerald No, probably not.
Bill Or listening to you? At all?
Susan No. We still keep his room for him. All his old things. His furniture. Equipment. Ridiculous.
Bill Yes, it hardly seems worth it, does it? Why is he bothering to come? If that's not a stupid question?
Gerald Well ...
Susan No. Good question. Not to see us, certainly. Why is he coming, Gerald? Did he say in his letter?
Gerald He—er ... (*To Bill*) He's allowed to write to us, you see——
Susan Gerald, why is he coming?
Gerald He—he asked me ... Well, he's in need of funds and he's——
Susan He's getting nothing from us. Not for that lot.
Gerald So he wants to sell all his personal possessions to raise money ...
Susan What personal possessions?
Gerald His things. In his room. He wants to sell his room.
Susan His room? He can't sell his room. You mean, the furniture?
Gerald I think that's the idea ...
Susan (*furiously*) You're going to let him sell his furniture? His desk? His bed? His swivel chair?
Gerald Well, I can't see how——
Susan I won't have it. You are not going to let him do that, Gerald. He can't sell them. They're things we gave him. They're our things. We gave them to him——
Gerald No, dearest, they're *his* things. We gave them to *him*. That makes them *his*. You see?
Susan (*suddenly deeply distressed*) But ... that's all that's left of him. If we sell ... his bed ... and his—swivel chair ... then he'll have gone completely. We'll have nothing left of him at all.
Gerald (*touching her arm rather ineffectually*) I'm sorry, dear ... I'm sorry ...
Susan I won't be able to sit in there, now. Like I do.
Gerald No. But I don't see how we can ...

They both stand miserably for a moment. Bill is appalled

Bill (*making a move*) Look, I've just remembered, I've got a——
Gerald Don't go, Bill. Please. We'd like you here. (*Trying to comfort Susan*) You know, it just occurred to me. Maybe he'll be allowed to talk to Muriel. She's not immediate family, is she? I don't know if they include aunts. We could try him with Muriel ...
Susan Who the hell would want to talk to Muriel?
Gerald (*lamely*) It might be worth a try ...
Bill What about—me? Would he talk to me?
Gerald Oh, yes, he'll talk to you. No problem there.
Bill In that case, if there's—anything you'd like me to ask him ... for you— I'll ...
Gerald Thank you, Bill. Thank you. We may call on you.

A slight pause. Susan, who has grown listless after her outburst, has wandered away from them again, leaving her sherry glass on the card table. In the course of her wanderings, she comes across her glass of champagne and drinks it

Susan (*dully*) Cheers.
Gerald More Marsala, anyone?
Bill No, no. This is perfect.
Gerald I think I might. I think I could. Is this your glass, Susan? You'll join me, won't you? Yes. (*He pours them both another*)

Muriel comes on, hot and flustered, with a bowl of nuts

Ah, Muriel. Everything in hand, is it?
Muriel Everything's in hand. (*Putting the bowl down*) Some nibbles. Susan, the herbs in the red tin by the tea pot? I couldn't be sure if they were thyme or sage.
Susan In the red tin?
Muriel Yes.
Susan That's Earl Grey Tea.
Muriel (*worried*) Earl Grey Tea. Right. (*Moving off*) I do wish you'd label things, Susan. It's a very inconvenient kitchen to work in, it really is ...

Muriel goes

Gerald Yes. Well. Good health.
Susan Cheers. (*She drains her Marsala*)
Gerald Steady, dear ...

Susan ignores him

You've got children of course, haven't you, Bill?
Bill Yes. Katie and Caroline. Caroline I think's going to be the doctor. She's at Guy's. And Katie's just got a music scholarship to Cambridge.
Susan (*miserably*) Lovely.
Gerald (*unhappily*) Yes.
Bill (*with embarrassment*) Both as thick as six bricks really. Like their parents. But they—seem to have muddled through. Somehow.

Muriel hurries back

Muriel He's here. Ricky's here. I heard the front doorbell. I had a look. It's him.
Gerald Did you let him in?
Muriel No, I——
Gerald Well, let him in, Muriel. We must let him in. Bill, I wonder if you'd mind——
Bill Do you want me to come?
Gerald If you would be so good. Just in case we need to communicate with each other ...
Bill Surely.
Gerald Thank you so much.
Muriel I hope he still likes omelettes ...

Bill and Muriel go

Gerald is on the point of following when he sees that Susan hasn't moved

Gerald Susan, are you coming?
Susan In a moment . . .
Gerald He's arrived. Rick's here.
Susan (*sharply*) In a minute, Gerald.
Gerald (*flustered*) All right. All right.

Gerald goes

Susan hesitates and then reluctantly makes to follow. As she does so . . .

Lucy appears

Lucy Mummy?
Susan (*without looking at her*) Oh, hallo, darling.
Lucy Are you coming to eat? Everything's ready . . .
Susan I can't today, darling, I'm sorry——
Lucy (*hurt*) What?
Susan I have to—have lunch somewhere else.
Lucy Somewhere else?
Susan Yes.
Lucy But what about us? What about the family? You can't leave us . . .
Susan (*rather desperate*) I'm sorry. Another time . . .

Lucy stands shattered. Susan turns to go, aware of the effect she has had upon her daughter. She nearly collides with . . .

Gerald as he returns

Gerald He's gone upstairs to his room. Bill says he says he'll be down in a minute . . .
Susan Have you seen Ricky yourself!
Gerald No. Not yet. Not personally. I heard him talking to Bill. I hid in the hall cupboard. Suddenly I lost my nerve and hid in the cupboard. Quite ridiculous. What if Rick had opened the door? What if he'd had a coat? Please come along, Susan. Please.
Susan Just give me a moment, Gerald.
Gerald I've given you ample moment, now come on.

Muriel enters

Muriel Are you all coming to the table or not? Things are starting to burn, you know . . .
Gerald All right, all right. (*With a despairing glance back as he goes*) Please, Susan . . .

Gerald and Muriel go out, Gerald taking the bottle and nuts with him

Susan (*making to take a step*) God, I think I'm drunk.

Tony enters with a small garden table, already laid for four, which he sets down on the grass

Tony Andy says that if no one is coming in to lunch, then lunch must come to you. Come on, young Lucy, shift yourself and give us a hand.
Lucy (*brightening*) Right.

Lucy hurries off

Tony (*to Susan*) One moment, madam. The waitress is fetching you a chair.
Susan No, I can't stop, Tony, I have to go ...
Tony What, with all that champagne to finish ...?
Susan Really ...

Lucy enters with two chairs which she sets at the table

Tony There we are, you see. Allow me ... (*He takes Susan's hand*)
Lucy Luncheon is served.
Susan (*pulling back*) No ... No. Why won't you understand? Why won't you let me go inside?
Tony (*letting go of her hand*) The truth? Because we love you and we don't want to see you hurt. If you want the truth.
Susan What are you talking about? What nonsense. Nobody's going to hurt me.
Lucy (*sadly*) They will, Mummy. They always do. Admit it.
Susan (*a moment's deliberation*) Very well, I'll eat with you.

She moves slowly to the table

Tony (*with a whoop*) I'll get the rest.

Tony goes off

Susan (*brightening immediately as she surveys the table*) Oh, doesn't this look pretty!
Lucy (*indicating the chair facing away from the house*) Here, Mummy, you sit here. You must have a view of the lake.

Susan is about to sit as ...

Bill enters

Bill (*tentatively*) Susan, I ...
Lucy (passing Susan, hissing) Tell him to go away.
Bill We were all wondering if you were coming in. We've all sat down, you see. And we were wondering if you were. Coming. In. Are you?

During this, Tony enters with two more chairs. Lucy has gone off momentarily

Tony Tell him to get lost.
Susan No, Bill, I'm not. I'm sorry. Can you explain to them I couldn't face being indoors, just at present?
Bill (*lingering*) Yes. OK. It's just——
Susan (*irritably*) What?

Lucy enters with three more champagne glasses and the bottle. During the next, she sets these, together with Susan's glass, on the table

Tony (*cheerfully*) Tell him take a jump ...
Bill Well, if you could see it from——
Lucy Mind his own business ...
Bill My point of view ...
Tony Drop dead.
Lucy Drop dead.
Bill I mean, I'm nothing to do with any of this. I'm just stuck in the middle.

I feel like an interpreter at some very, very hostile summit conference ...
Frankly, Susan, it's a very large price to pay for an omelette. So. Please.
Susan Oh, Bill, do drop dead.
Bill (*after a slight pause, crushed*) Fair enough.

Bill goes off

Tony That's telling him.
Lucy Nice one, Mummy ... Now, do sit down.
Tony Yes, sit down.
Susan Yes. (*She sits slowly, still rather shocked at what she has said to Bill*) I must be terribly drunk. That's the only excuse I have.

Andy enters with a dish of elaborately garnished and decorated cold salmon

Andy (*with a flourish*) Tarrah!
Tony Oh, just take a look at that!
Lucy Fabulous!

Lucy and Tony applaud as Andy sets the dish down. Susan is still rather bewildered

What do you think of that, Mother?
Susan (*faintly*) Wonderful. Thank you.
Andy There was an unkind rumour flying around my kitchen at one point that you were about to be tempted away from all this by a mere omelette. I trust that wasn't true?
Susan No ...
Tony (*filling their glasses*) False alarm.
Lucy All lies, Daddy ...
Andy I should hope so. I'd have been totally grief-stricken for days ... (*Raising his glass*) Well, here's to it, then. To us all. The family.
All The family!

They toast each other

Andy I know what I wanted to ask. Have we heard any news from Cambridge about your music scholarship, Lucy?
Lucy Nope. Not a word, yet.
Tony She'll get it. She's brilliant.
Andy Not if she doesn't practise, she won't——
Lucy I do practise.
Andy Really? Have you seen that cello of yours lately, young lady? It's got about three inches of dust on it. Mrs Simmonds nearly hoovered it up twice ...

They all laugh. Susan manages a smile, aware they're trying to cheer her up

Lucy (*laughing*) Honestly, Daddy, that's a total exaggeration. I practised on Tuesday——
Tony (*shouting her down*) No, you didn't——
Lucy I did! And on Thursday ...
Andy Not Thursday. You were out with me on Thursday ...
Lucy Only in the afternoon——
Tony Rubbish! Rubbish! All rubbish!

As their voices reach a cacophonous peak, Rick enters unobtrusively from the direction of the house. He is in his early twenties. Contrary perhaps to expectations, there is nothing at all extraordinary or alarming about his appearance. He is dressed casually, suggesting a person with little or no interest in his personal appearance

Rick (*softly*) Mum . . .

Andy, who is facing that way, is the first to see Rick. He stops and stares. The others, noting Andy's expression, follow suit. Susan is the last to turn

Mum?

Susan (*stunned*) Rick? (*She gets up, rather unsteadily. She stares at her son unbelievingly*) Ricky? Is that you? Speaking?

Rick Yes. We wondered if you were coming in for lunch?

Susan Oh, yes. Yes, of course . . . (*She starts to make her way, somewhat uncertainly, towards the house*)

The family continue to stare

Rick Can you manage?

Susan Yes. Oh, yes. (*She reaches the middle of the garden and sways*) I wonder—I wonder if one of you would be so good as to hold on to me for a moment?

Rick (*moving to steady her*) Mum?

Susan I just feel a little sleepy. I'll be fine in a—— (*As her knees begin to buckle under her*) Oh, no . . . Here I go again . . .

As she falls, Rick catches her. We hear her long drawn-out cry. She sinks into a drink-induced oblivion, causing a Black-out

CURTAIN

ACT II

Darkness

We hear the sound of Susan's groan as she comes out of her swoon. As she opens her eyes, the Lights come up. It is a few seconds later. She is lying on the grass rather as at the start of the play, only this time Rick is bending over her

Rick Mum?

Susan stares at him

Mum?

Susan (*bemused*) Ricky? (*She sits up with difficulty*) Ricky? I dreamt you spoke to me. Are you speaking to me? Is it you?

Rick Yes, it's me. It's Rick speaking.

Susan What's happened? (*Smiling*) It must be Mother's Day. Or have you got special dispensation?

Rick No, I've left the group.

Susan You have? When?

Rick Oh—three months ago. Something like that.

Susan Why didn't you come and see us before?

Rick I had one or two things to sort out.

Susan Oh. I see. Well, I don't know what your reasons for leaving were, but I can't pretend that I'm not delighted at the news. If it means we'll be able to see you occasionally. Talk to you like a normal human being.

Rick (*non-committally*) Yes.

Susan Where are you living now? Not still in Hemel Hempstead?

Rick No, I've moved back into London. South London.

Susan I see. And so? What are you doing? Have you got a job?

Rick Not just at present, no.

Susan Must be difficult, then? Making ends meet? Oh, this feels so odd talking to you—like a stranger. Do you have a room in South London?

Rick No, we've got a flat.

Susan We?

Rick Me and this girl.

Susan Oh? You've got a girl-friend?

Rick Well, she's more than that, really.

Susan (*smiling rather coyly*) A lover, then?

Rick No. Really, more of a wife, really . . .

Susan (*blankly*) A wife?

Rick Yeah.

Susan You're married.

Rick Yeah.

Susan When? When did you marry?

Rick About two months ago. Tess, she was with the group, too and—we both decided we'd had enough really. I mean, we'd got what we could from it . . .

Susan Yes, yes . . .

Rick And we felt we'd grown, you know, through it.

Susan Yes. Good. Yes.

Rick So we left. And we thought maybe we should give things a week or two, you know, just to see them in perspective. You know?

Susan Yes.

Rick And—things seemed OK so we got married. You know.

Susan Where?

Rick Where?

Susan Where did you get married?

Rick Some registry office, I can't——

Susan Which one?

Rick (*slightly irritably*) I don't know which one, Mum. It doesn't matter, does it?

Susan No, no. No. (*After a slight pause*) You didn't even tell us. Send us a— card.

Rick No.

Susan And you haven't brought her with you . . .

Rick No.

Susan Tess? That's her name?

Rick Yeah.

Susan Did you have to get married? Was she . . . ?

Rick No, of course she wasn't. We wouldn't have got married just because of that.

Susan Then why did you?

Rick Why does anybody? We love each other.

Susan Oh, yes. Of course. I just thought perhaps——

Rick What?

Susan You'd got married as another way to get back at us. Your father and me. Silly idea, is it?

Rick It's a bloody ridiculous idea.

Susan Yes. (*She sits up with a little cry of grief*) Oh . . . sorry. I'll be all right in a moment.

Rick (*muttering*) I knew you'd take it like this——

Susan Well, what did you expect?

Lucy appears at a distance from them

Lucy (*calling softly*) Mother . . . Mother . . .

Susan Oh, do go away . . .

Rick What?

Susan Nothing.

Lucy, a little hurt, sits at some distance from them and watches unobtrusively

You haven't told your father yet, I take it?

Rick No.

Susan What on earth's he going to say?

Rick Quite a lot, probably. Not a man of few words when several spring to mind, is he?

Susan (*laughing*) Oh, that's very good, Ricky. Sums him up exactly. When I think what he and I could have achieved with our lives if he hadn't insisted on discussing everything first ... (*brightening*) Well, we must make up for lost time, mustn't we? The first thing is to meet Tess. Get to know her. You must both come and stay, that's what you must do.

Rick No, the point is that Tess is a trained nurse, you know, and she's got this offer of a job. Overseas.

Susan Overseas?

Rick Yes. So we'll probably both be going pretty soon.

Susan Where?

Rick Thailand.

Susan Thailand? (*Blankly*) That's miles.

Rick Yes.

Susan (*distressed again*) Oh, Ricky ... What are *you* going to do there? In Thailand? While she's—nursing?

Rick I don't know. Help out, you know. Sort of odd-job man, probably.

Susan Do they have odd-job men in Thailand?

Rick They soon will do.

Susan So we aren't even going to meet this—Tess? Tess. Not a terribly attractive name, is it? Tess. A bit lumpen, isn't it? Are we going to see her or not?

Rick No. It's not possible this time round. I'll be staying a couple of days. I'm planning to sell off a few old things of mine. Raise a bit of spare cash. Then we're both off at the end of next week.

Susan Well, she could come down while you were here, couldn't she?

Rick No, she's got her own stuff to sort out, you see.

Susan She could come for the day? For lunch?

Rick I'd rather she didn't.

Susan You would?

Rick Yeah. I don't really want her coming here yet.

Susan Why? Because of your father? Well, we can keep him out of the way, can't we? They need hardly meet at all. Don't worry, I'll arrange things ...

Rick It's only partly Dad.

Susan Well, who else? (*After a slight pause*) Me?

Rick Yeah. Just a bit. Sorry.

Susan You don't want me to meet her?

Rick No. Not yet. Maybe in a couple of years. We'll see.

Susan A couple of years? What am I supposed to do? Fly out to Thailand for tea? Don't be ridiculous. Why can't I meet her now?

Rick I can't go into it now, Mum. I'd just rather you didn't, that's all.

Susan I feel I have a right to know why.

Rick Because—Tess is fairly—well ... I suppose you'd call her unsophisticated, in a way. And a bit shy. With people.

Susan Gauche, I think, is the word you're looking for.

Rick No, not gauche. She looks at things simply, that's all. She's straightforward. I just don't think she could cope with you. Not with your attitude.

Susan What attitude?

Rick Well ... I remember how you used to be with girls I used to bring home.

Susan I remember, too. We got on terribly well.

Rick No, you didn't, Mum. I mean, frankly, you used to embarrass the hell out of them. Didn't you know that?

Susan Nonsense.

Rick You did. You used to get them into corners and start going on about—I don't know—contraception methods and multiple orgasms ... I mean, I'd hardly even kissed them, you were asking them for their medical histories.

Susan Nonsense, they were sixteen, seventeen-year-old girls who needed to know these things ... I wasn't having a woman going out with a son of mine who didn't know what she was about. You'd have thanked me for it later ... You? You didn't know a thing till I told you.

Rick Yes, I did. We all did. It's just we didn't necessarily want to sit down and talk to you about it. I mean, if you started on like that with Tess she'd die.

Susan All right, I won't.

Rick You will.

Susan I promise.

Rick You will. Because you can't help it. You always want to finish up being girl-friends with them, that's what it is.

Susan Better than some mother-in-laws. Deadly rivals.

Rick Maybe that's healthier.

Susan Don't be so silly. Right. Your lecture is noted and understood. Thank you. All through your childhood I embarrassed the life out of you. Well, may I say from my side, Ricky, I think you are selfish, insensitive and priggish.

Rick doesn't reply

Mention the word sex to you, you go pink round the ears. Just like your father. I presume that's the reason you buried yourself in Hemel Hempstead. Was it? With that bunch of cranks. To avoid me?

No reply

Obviously, from that, I assume it was. Wonderful. So I've been a total failure, have I? As a mother as well as a——

Rick Nobody said that.

Susan It's a shame you told me that. Up to now, I always thought I'd managed rather well. I should have had a daughter. I could have coped with her. (*Rather waspishly*) Boys are all such delicate blossoms, aren't they?

Lucy looks up

Rick I don't want to hurt you any more, Mum, but God help any daughter who had you as a mother.

A pause

Look, don't take it all personally. It wasn't just you. There was Dad as well. Looking them all up and down. Terrified they'd turn out to be the daughters of Beelzebub. Scarlet women after his son's body. Tess came straight to the group from a convent education and training. She knows all about the theory of life. Don't worry. But she's still a bit short on the practical. And she needs to be introduced to certain elements of it gradually. Elements like you and Dad.

Susan It's no use. You can be as loyal to your father as you like. I know which one of us was really responsible for all this . . .

Rick (*wearily*) Mum . . .

Gerald comes from the house

Gerald Ah, you're here! We all wondered where you—(*he suppresses a burp*)—wondered where you'd vanished off to. Bill's gone. I think the combination of potential family traumas and Muriel's cooking proved altogether too much for the poor man. (*Another suppressed burp*) I beg your pardon. You know that really was quite the most appalling meal I've ever tasted. I'd forgotten how bad she was. Burnt Earl Grey omelettes. It's almost an art form to mistreat food in that way.

Rick How long's she staying?

Gerald Just until she——

Susan For ever.

Gerald —finds someone else to share her cooking, I suppose. Yes, probably for ever. Still, what are we to do? She's no huge problem. She spends most of her life trying vainly to contact her late husband, where's the harm?

Tony wanders on. He is dressed for the shoot. A twelve-bore shotgun (loaded but broken open) over his arm. An empty bag for game slung over his shoulder

Susan watches him

You two been having a heart to heart? Have I missed anything? Any startling news?

Susan (*looking at him, acidly*) Quite a bit, I'd say.

Gerald What's that dreadful look supposed to mean? Eh? If looks could kill . . . (*He laughs*)

Susan looks away

I take it there's some problem. Rick, is there a problem?

Rick I think I'll leave Mum to tell you, Dad. (*Going*) I must start sorting out my stuff . . .

Gerald Just as you wish, son. Just as you wish.

Rick goes off to the house

(*Calling after him*) If you need the receipts for anything I probably still have them. (*More to himself*) Probably. Filed away.

Susan F for furniture. F for family.

Gerald Are you going to tell me, then? Rick's news?

Susan Yes, of course. What would you like to hear about first? His runaway registry office wedding? His wife? Mouselike Tess, the nervous nursing novice. His forthcoming trip to Thailand? His——

Gerald Just a minute. Just a minute. Thailand?

Susan Thailand. (*Waving vaguely*) It's over there . . .

Tony (*helpfully indicating*) That way.

Susan That way. Somewhere. Past India.

Gerald (*irritably*) Yes, I know where Thailand is. Why's he going there? As a missionary?

Susan As an odd-job man, so I understand.

Gerald I don't quite follow all this. You say he has a wife?

Susan A bride of two months.

Gerald Why didn't he tell us?

Susan I should have thought that was fairly obvious.

Gerald Yes. I suppose so. All the same, I don't think it's fair to lay all the blame at your door . . .

Tony What?

Lucy What?

Susan What?

Gerald There are probably two sides.

Lucy Mother, don't stand for this . . .

Susan My door? Did I hear you correctly?

Lucy Her door?

Susan My door?

Tony Want me to shoot him?

Susan No.

Gerald No, I'm saying, there are usually two sides——

Susan How dare you?

Lucy How dare he?

Tony Perfectly easy to shoot him . . .

Susan (*to Tony*) No. (*To Gerald*) How dare you stand there and——

Gerald Now, Susan, I'm not going to start on this. We have argued our lives away over that boy and we're not going to do it any more. I refuse to become involved——

Susan You smug——

Lucy Self-satisfied——

Susan Self-satisfied——

Tony Conceited——

Susan Conceited . . . bastard!

Lucy and Tony cheer and applaud this last effort of Susan's

Gerald (*wagging a finger admonishingly*) Ah-ah-ah-ah! Ah-ah-ah-ah! Now. Now.

Susan (*softer*) Bastard!

Muriel comes on carrying a tray with four coffee cups

Muriel Here comes a lovely cup of coffee.

Gerald (*startled*) What?

Tony Yurk. I'll see you later.

Tony exits

Susan No, thank you, Muriel.

Gerald Ah. No, no, no, no, Muriel. Thanks. Enough is as good as— enough. Thank you.

Muriel No?

Gerald I must get back to my labours.

Susan That's right. Back to your bloody book.

Muriel (*shocked*) Now, now, now, Susan. That's no way to talk to him.

Gerald It's all right, Muriel. Susan is a little—(*he suppresses a burp*)—she's just a little bit—(*another burp*)—would you excuse me, I've got the most terrible ... Excuse me.

Gerald hurries off

Muriel (*concerned*) Now look what you've done? Shouting at him like that. You've given him indigestion ... The trouble with you is, Susan, you never learnt how to treat a man properly ...

Susan (*sarcastically*) I don't know what you know about these things, Muriel, I'm sure ...

Muriel goes off after Gerald, cluckingly concerned

(*Yelling after her angrily*) Don't blame me. Blame your poisonous omelettes ... (*Muttering*) Everyone's blaming me. Everyone. For everything.

Lucy now moves closer to Susan, comfortingly

Lucy Mother? ... Mummy, don't be unhappy. (*Kneeling by Susan*) Can we talk about my wedding?

Susan (*rather more curtly than normal*) Yes, we will do, darling, but not just at this moment.

Lucy Even if they don't appreciate you, we love you, Mother.

Susan Yes, thank you, darling.

Lucy I think you're just the most marvellous person—ever. Do you know what it said in the *Sunday Times* about you, last week? It said you were the most brilliant woman heart surgeon there was in this country. It said——

Susan (*snapping*) Oh, do shut up, Lucy. For heaven's sake, don't be so stupid. I'm not a heart surgeon. I never have been. Now go away.

Lucy (*hurt*) Yes, Mother.

Her eyes brimming with tears, she rises and rushes away

Susan (*immediately remorseful*) Oh, I'm sorry. I'm sorry. Come back. I'm sorry.

Gerald enters from the other direction

Gerald (*as he does so*) All right! Apology accepted.

Susan I wasn't——

Gerald Mmmm?

Susan Nothing. What do you want?

Gerald I have returned for my card table. I need it in my study for my pages. Oh, by the way, Mrs Ogle telephoned me from next door. An operation which involved us both in a great deal of shouting. She's apparently lost her dog. Spike. You haven't seen Spike, have you? It hasn't got in here?

Susan No.

Gerald Probably in the road. Under a truck. Right. (*He makes to leave*)

Susan Gerald ...

Gerald (*turning back*) Mmm?

Susan You don't feel we should perhaps talk.

Gerald No. I don't quite honestly. I don't at all. I think talking has got us precisely nowhere. East is East. Never the twain shall meet. Jack Spratt could eat no fat. We beg to differ.

Susan You put everything so well, Gerald. No wonder you're a writer.

Gerald I think I detect sarcasm. I can't be doing with sarcasm. You know what they say? Sarcasm is the greatest weapon of the smallest mind. I'll see you at tea-time.

Susan If you leave me now for that damn—book, I warn you, Gerald, you will have nailed up the final—door—in our relationship ...

Gerald Nailed up the final door? What is this nonsense? (*He turns and goes*)

Susan You will have dug that final yard of moat between us!

Gerald (*in the distance*) Rubbish! Rubbish!

Gerald has gone

Susan (*still ploughing on*) You will have—you will have uncoiled the final strands of electrified barbed wire that serve to keep us—— (*Giving up*) Oh, what's the use?

She is alone now. She stares at the sky and listens. The garden grows darker as though moving towards sunset

After a moment, Andy appears and watches her

Susan does not look at him

Andy Beautiful, isn't it? The sunset?

Susan (*without turning*) Yes, we're very lucky. Having all this.

Andy (*moving closer to her*) I hear you were angry with Lucy.

Susan I'm sorry. Did she tell you?

Andy She only wanted to please you.

Susan I know, I know ...

Andy Her whole world falls apart when you do that——

Susan All right, Andy, don't keep on at me. I'm sorry.

Andy (*kissing the back of her neck*) Forgiven.

Susan (*wriggling with pleasure*) Mmmm. How do you make me feel so helpless? You only have to touch me and my knees give way ...

Andy laughs

Tony strolls into view, returning from his shoot. His bloodstained game bag now contains something freshly killed

Tony Hi! It's a lovely evening for doing whatever it is you look as if you're both thinking of doing ...

Andy On your way, callow youth. Any luck?

Tony Just one. (*He holds up the bag*)

Andy Well, better than nothing.

Susan What is it? What have you shot?

Tony Nothing, old love. Just a rodent.

Susan What sort of rodent?

Tony (*shrugging*) A rodent's a rodent, isn't it?

Susan I want to see.
Tony (*wandering off*) I'll show you later . . .
Andy He'll show you later.
Tony Once it's skinned and cooked . . . See you.

Tony wanders off

Susan Andy, what has he just killed?
Andy Oh, darling, how should I know? He shoots anything that moves. You know Tony.
Susan (*drawing back from him a little*) No, I don't think I do know Tony. Not any more. Any more than I think I know you. You've altered. You've all altered, recently.
Andy Darling . . . Come on.
Susan What do you want from me? What are you doing here?
Andy You know that . . .
Susan No, I don't. What?
Andy We're here because you asked us here.
Susan No. That's just the point, you see. That was how it was, originally. Yes. I whistled and you came. Yes. But not now. You just keep popping up. All of you. That girl. She's taken to just coming and sitting there, now, staring at me for ages on end——
Andy That girl's your daughter.
Susan Well, whoever. I was having a private conversation. Why was she sitting there?
Andy She felt you needed her.
Susan Well, I didn't. I was perfectly able to cope. And now Tony's started. Chipping in when I'm talking to someone.
Andy If you don't want them, tell them to go away. They'll go. You've only to tell us. Any of us.
Susan Well, I am. I'm telling you now. Please go.

Andy doesn't move

Go on. Shoo. Vanish.

He smiles at her but still doesn't move

There you are, you see. You don't take a blind bit of notice of me, do you? I've told you to go. You're still here.
Andy Perhaps you didn't really mean it?
Susan Of course I meant it. I want to see Gerald now. Go away. I'm going to have a chat with Gerald about his book. It's absolutely riveting, you know. It's all about the parish since thirteen eighty-six. Did you know that until eighteen seventy-four there used to be sheep grazing where the town hall is now? I bet you didn't know that. Or I might just pop upstairs and embarrass my son and discuss sexually transmitted diseases with him. Or help Muriel make a soap-flake soup. (*Desperately*) What do you want from me? Just tell me. What do you all want?
Andy Or—put another way . . .
Susan What other way?
Andy There is no——
Susan There is no——

Andy—other way to——
Susan —other way to——
Andy—why are you——
Susan—why are you——
Andy —saying everything——
Susan —saying everything——
Andy —before I do?
Susan —before I do?
Andy Oh!
Susan (*with an angry cry of frustration*) Oh!
Andy Or put another way—why are you repeating everything I say?

Susan opens and closes her mouth but decides not to speak

Go on, say it. (*Prompting her*) Oh, God! What's happening to me?
Susan (*with a wail*) Oh, God! What's happening to me?
Andy There are all sorts of games we can play, you see. With our minds.
Susan Go away. Please, go away.
Andy (*teasing*) Ah, now wait. Is that you telling me to go away or could that be me telling you to go away? It's sometimes hard to tell, isn't it?
Susan Please . . .
Andy (*adopting her tone*) Andy, I'm warning you . . .
Susan (*adopting his tone*) Warning me of what exactly, Susie?
Andy (*as Susan*) That if you don't . . . if you don't leave me . . . alone . . . Andy?
Susan (*as Andy*) Anything wrong, Susie?
Andy (*as Susan*) Oh, God! Where am I? Where have I gone?
Susan (*as Andy*) You're over here.
Andy (*as Susan*) No, I'm not. I'm over here . . .
Susan (*as Tony*) Where?
Andy (*as Susan*) Who's that? Is that you, Lucy?
Susan (*as Tony*) No, this is Tony.
Andy (*as Susan*) Andy! Andy!
Susan (*as Lucy*) Daddy? I'm here.
Andy (*as Tony*) Hi! Big Sis?
Susan (*as Lucy*) Mummy! Where are you? I'm frightened.
Andy (*as Susan*) I'm here, darling, I'm here.
Susan (*as Susan*) No, I'm here. (*As Lucy*) Mummy? (*As Susan*) No, there.
Andy (*as Lucy*) Mummy?
Susan (*as Susan*) No, everywhere. (*As Lucy*) Mummy? (*As Susan*) Oh God, I'm everywhere. What am I doing everywhere . . . It's like not . . . (*Slowly*) . . . Not being—anywhere. Where am I? Where am I now?
Andy (*as Tony*) It's all right Susie, you're there.
Susan I'm here?
Andy Home where you belong.
Susan (*staring at him in horror*) Who are you? Really?

Andy smiles

Oh, no. You go away. You keep away from me.
Andy (*laughing*) Beware, Susie! Nothing is who it is! No-one is what he seems!

He goes. The sunset is replaced by a normal mild afternoon light

Susan looks about her apprehensively

Susan (*to herself, pleased*) They've gone. They have. They've all gone. Good. (*Shouting*) Don't come back, any of you. Ever. I don't want you, do you hear? Go away and stay away for ever.

Bill has entered unobtrusively behind her, carrying his case

Bill (*cheerily*) Hallo. Does that include me?

Susan jumps with a stifled scream

Sorry.
Susan Oh, Bill. How glad I am to see you.
Bill Really?
Susan Really. You're just the person I need. Someone calm and unflappable and *sane* ...
Bill Thanks very much. I don't think I've ever been called that before. Well, not all three in the same breath, anyway ...
Susan I thought you'd left after lunch.
Bill Yes, I did. I'm sorry. It was just there was some talk of a dessert and I'm afraid I lost my nerve. Then halfway home I thought, this won't do. What about you? What about my patient? So I'm back. Because frankly, I'm still a fraction concerned about you, if you must know. You still seem a mite keyed up. Oh—(*fumbling in his pocket*)—and I brought you these—(*he produces a bottle of pills*)—which I already had. They might do the trick. They're fairly mild but if you can't sleep they may help. OK?
Susan May I ask you a question?
Bill I know what you're going to ask. Not more than four over twenty-four hours.
Susan No, that wasn't what I was going to ask——
Bill Ah. Wrong again. Yes?
Susan It's this. (*She hesitates*) Well ... Difficult to put without sounding absurd but ... Do you believe that in this day and age it's possible for someone to be possessed?
Bill Possessed?
Susan Yes.
Bill You mean by demons? That sort of thing?
Susan That sort of thing.
Bill That's a—that's a bit out of my league, really. I mean, I'm not ducking the question—well, yes, I am ducking the question but—— Why don't you ask Gerald? He's our man on the spot, surely?
Susan No, I don't want to ask Gerald. I'm asking you.
Bill (*deliberating*) Well. The answer to that is ... My answer to that is—like most of my answers to important questions, I'm afraid—is possibly, but I don't really know. It's a bit like—what?—"Is there life on other planets?" The scientists say, "Look here, we've just discovered X billion billion stars, Y billion billion of which certainly have planetary systems. And of these, Z billion billion have almost certainly got earth-type atmospheres, probably supporting life as we know it." So you look up at the sky and what do you see? Bugger all. Pardon the language. I mean according to

those chaps, the sky up there should look like a beach at Bank Holiday.
Absolutely teeming with little men dashing hither and thither. And
instead, absolutely empty. But that's not to say scientists are wrong. But
they could be. Sorry. So getting back to you. The answer's possibly. Why
do you ask?

Susan It's just that I think I might be.

Bill You? Possessed?

Susan It's possible.

Bill Good Lord. Truly?

Susan You know I told you that I had these hallucinations a while back?

Bill You mean yesterday?

Susan Yesterday? Was it yesterday . . . Well, the thing is, they haven't gone.
I said they had but they haven't. They're still with me. Only more
frequently.

Bill I see. I see (*He ponders*) Do they—er—do they happen at any particular
time? Of the day? Of the month? After meals, say?

Susan (*rather coolly*) I don't think they're a result of an upset stomach if
that's what you're asking.

Bill No, no. Fair enough. Just a shot in the dark. Sometimes these . . . You
don't drink that much alcohol, do you?

Susan (*cooler still*) No.

Bill Not on any sort of drugs, are you?

Susan Only what you've just given me.

Bill Yes. Well. You'll have your work cut out to hallucinate on those. No, it
seems to me it's either our old friend the garden rake. Or . . .

Susan Or?

Bill It really is something you ought to talk to Gerald about.

Susan I couldn't talk to Gerald. Not possibly——

Bill If not as a vicar, at least as your husband.

Susan That would be even worse. It would be like—undressing in front of
him. *You* must understand, surely? Isn't it the case that some doctors'
wives prefer not to consult their own husbands? Isn't that true?

Bill Oh yes, quite common. Nora doesn't use me. She always goes to my
partner. Geoff Burgess. Quite frequently, actually. I mean she looks
perfectly fit to me, blooming. But she keeps finding all sorts of things
wrong with her. Still . . .

Susan Yes. Reverting to me, if we could . . .

Bill I'm sorry. That's my problem, you see. I think as a doctor I'm perfectly
sound, it's just that——

Susan (*interrupting*) It's just that the only alternative to all this, Bill, is that
I'm going off my head . . .

Bill Oh. No, no. Lord, no . . .

Susan Are you sure?

Bill Absolutely, positive. Listen, I've seen countless people going off their
heads on several occasions and they were nothing like you . . . You're
perfectly fine. Probably a bit run down, that's all.

Susan Seeing things that nobody else sees? Are those the symptoms of
someone who's just a bit run down?

Bill Possibly, possibly . . .

Susan Holding conversations with people who might not be there?

Bill Yes, it's all—theoretically feasible ...

Susan (*agitated*) If only someone else saw them. Then I'd know I was sane——

Bill Quite.

Susan But nobody else is going to, are they? Because they're all in my head.

She paces about in a feverish manner. Bill watches her with increasing anxiety

I know ... that somehow ... like those genies that live in bottles, you know ... If I can only keep them from getting out ... I'll be all right. They mustn't get out ... Whatever happens ...

Bill Do you think that's wise ... ?

Susan Why not?

Bill Well, surely, don't you feel that these—whatever they are—are merely a symptom of something else?

Susan They are?

Bill Almost certainly. And with any symptoms—I'm not a psychiatrist—but with any medical symptom, it can be a dangerous thing to suppress it. Or try and ignore it. A symptom is simply something trying to signal. Something. Put very simply. Try to suppress it and you're putting your thumb over the valve of a pressure cooker.

Susan Yes, yes ...

Bill (*gaining in confidence as his theory takes shape*) At worst, there'll be an almighty explosion and a great deal of damage. Even at best, you're liable to finish up with your dinner all over the ceiling.

Susan It's wrong to bottle things up, then?

Bill Dangerous.

Susan But if I let them out, these people, I don't know that I can control them. Not any more.

Bill Don't worry, Susan. I'm going to fix an appointment with someone for you. I know a good, reliable chap. And we'll fight it. If necessary we'll fight them off together.

Susan (*touched by his concern*) Oh, Bill ... How can you fight something you can't see? It's up to me.

Bill I can help.

Susan If you could see them you could.

Bill If I could, would it help?

Susan Oh, yes. Of course it would.

A pause. Bill looks around

Bill They're—are they here at the moment?

Susan No.

Bill No? Oh, good. (*With a relieved laugh*) I was going to say, if they are here, I can't see them.

A pause

Muriel comes on from the house, whistling rather feebly

They stare at her

Muriel Spikey! You haven't seen him, have you?

Bill Sorry?

Muriel Mrs Ogle's little Spike? She's lost him.

Susan (*rather guiltily*) Has she?

Muriel Funny. He usually comes if you whistle him. Must have run off . . .
Want a cup of tea, either of you?

Bill (*hastily*) No, thank you.

Susan (*equally hastily*) No thanks.

Muriel Really? You sure?

Susan (*nastily*) You can make one for Gerald. He'd love one.

Muriel I'm going to. Spikey! Spikey!

Muriel goes off whistling

Bill Tea. That was a near thing. (*He laughs*)

Susan laughs with him. Bill feels encouraged

Your son seems very nice.

Susan Ricky? Oh, yes.

Bill (*laughing*) Not as bad as you feared, then? I presume?

Susan No, no. Thankfully.

Bill Left that place he was at?

Susan Yes.

Bill And what's he going to do now?

Susan Well . . . He's just told us some wonderful news, actually. We were
very thrilled.

Bill Oh, what's that?

Susan He's getting married.

Bill Oh super. Presentable, is she?

Susan How do you mean?

Bill The girl he's going to marry? That's always the big hurdle, isn't it? Who
are they going to lumber you with as an in-law? Our two girls, they've
both gone and settled for these awful whizz-kid stockbrokers. Dreadful
wheeler-dealers with their hair curling over their ears. Socialists with
Swiss bank accounts, you know the sort. Boring as hell. How's your
daughter-in-law-to-be, then?

Susan She's—all right. Not striking, you know. Quite plain, but . . .

Bill Ah.

Susan Got one of those heavy faces. Bit jowly. Or it will be, when she's
forty.

Bill Uh-huh.

Susan And that terribly fine hair that you can never quite do anything with.
You just want to grab hold of it and cut it all off. Poor girl.

Bill (*sympathetically*) Yes. Yes.

Susan Quite a thickset build——

Bill Well, so long as she's nice . . .

Susan Oh, yes. She's a dormouse.

Bill Are they moving in locally?

Susan No. They're off to the Far East, actually.

Bill That sounds exciting. How come?

Susan Well—Ricky has a job lined up there.

Bill Marvellous.

Susan And she's a Thai, actually.

Bill Yes, well, they can be, can't they?

Susan No, she's from Thailand. A Thai.

Bill Oh, heavens. Sorry. Yes.

Susan But as I say she's hardly that sparkling.

Bill Perhaps it's when she's with you. Maybe she feels a little bit outshone?

Susan (*modestly*) Oh . . .

Bill I don't know. You do tend to—I don't know.

Susan What?

Bill Well—linger on in the memory. You know.

Susan Oh, really . . .

Bill Yes, you do. It's a good job I'm not your regular doctor, isn't it? Otherwise that'd sound rather unethical.

Susan Don't be so silly.

Bill No, I do. I find you very attractive. And I have done for a very long time.

Susan You only met me—when was it?—yesterday.

Bill We've met before that.

Susan Occasionally.

Bill Quite occasionally. We never spoke to each other much, but I used to watch you. Talking to other people.

Susan Did you?

Bill Oh, yes.

Susan When?

Bill Oh, you know. At social things. Like—well, I remember the school concerts, particularly.

Susan School concerts?

Bill At Bilbury Lodge. You remember. All our kids leaping about in woolly animal ears, singing dreadful songs . . .

Susan That was ten years ago.

Bill Eleven. I know. Years.

Susan Well. Honestly.

Bill Sorry. I should never have told you, should I?

Susan No.

Bill I'm sorry.

Susan I'm glad you did though. (*She smiles*)

Bill smiles back. He looks at her and decides whether or not to kiss her. As he moves in gently . . .

Behind him, Lucy wanders on. She watches

Susan, naturally, sees her. She places her hand on Bill's shoulder to stop him

(*Softly*) Bill!

Bill What?

Susan She's here now. One of them's here now.

Bill You mean one of your——

Susan Yes. She's over there.

Bill (*turning cautiously*) Oh, yes?

Susan Can you see her . . . ? Please God, you can see her . . . Can you see anything?

Bill (*try as he might*) Not . . . immediately.

Susan If only you could see her, everything would be all right. I know it. (*Pointing*) She's there. She's just there.

Lucy Mother?

Susan There. That's my daughter. That's Lucy.

Bill (*staring at the spot where Susan's pointing*) Lucy.

Susan Do you see?

Bill Keep describing her.

Susan She's—quite tall. She's wearing a light-coloured dress and she's barefoot. Fair hair . . .

Bill Hang on. Yes, yes. I see her.

Susan You do? Kneeling down . . .

Bill Yes, kneeling down. She's very pretty.

Lucy kneels

Susan Oh, yes . . .

Bill moves towards Lucy. Though he can't see her, he makes a good stab at pretending he can. He crouches slightly to one side of Lucy and talks to the air

Bill (*quite avuncular*) Hallo, there. You're a big girl, aren't you? How old are you, then?

Lucy stares at him mystified

Bless my soul! Is that all? You look older than that. You must have been eating a lot of green vegetables.

Lucy (*getting up*) Mother?

Bill They make you grow up big and strong, did you know that? Did your mummy ever tell you that? I bet she did.

Lucy (*moving to Susan and leaving Bill happily chattering away*) Mother, who is he? What does he want?

Susan Nothing, darling. You're not to worry. He's just someone who—sees things . . .

Lucy How extraordinary. Is he mad?

Susan Possibly. One of us is anyway. And I'd sooner it were him.

Lucy Well, it certainly isn't you. Tell him to go away. He's untidying our beautiful garden.

Bill has been pretending to listen to his version of Lucy. He now responds to something she has said. Under the next, he keeps up a background conversation performing a conjuring trick with his pocket handkerchief to amuse her

Bill (*under the next*) Do you like spinach? Oh, you must eat your spinach. All little girls should eat up their spinach. And their lettuce. Do you eat your lettuce? Are you like a rabbit? Rabbits like lettuce, did you know that? Have you seen a rabbit round here? Wait a minute! Just a minute! I believe I have . . . (*fumbling in his pocket*) . . . yes, I do have—a rabbit in my pocket. (*He produces his handkerchief with a flourish*) Hey presto! What do you mean, this isn't a rabbit? Of course it's a rabbit. Wait! Wait! I'll show you. You see, we knot this . . . like this and then . . . this . . . like this and—look! There's a rabbit. Bo! Where's he gone now? Bo! . . . *etc etc.*

Tony enters and stares at Bill suspiciously

Tony What's that chap doing here?

Lucy Mother says he's a madman. Tell him to go away, Tony.

Tony Want me to chuck him out, Big Sis?

Susan No, don't. He's not doing any harm, really.

Tony What's he doing? Who's he talking to?

Lucy He's so ugly, Mummy. He's so terribly ugly.

Susan No, now you really mustn't call him that. He's been saying very
    sweet things to me . . .

Tony (*his eyes narrowing*) Sweet things? What sort of sweet things?

Susan Oh, just nice flattering things. Loving things.

Lucy (*scandalized*) How dare he?

Tony Right. That settles it, I'm going to shoot him . . .

Lucy Oh, good!

Susan No, no!

Bill carries on blissfully unaware of the danger he is in

  Andy enters at this point and surveys the scene

  (*Running to him*) Andy, stop them. Do stop them. They're behaving most
  terribly badly.

Andy What's going on, kids?

Lucy Daddy, that man's been saying awful, filthy things to Mummy. You
    must get rid of him . . .

Tony (*simultaneously with her*) Look, I'll go and fetch the twelve-bore. It
    won't take a second . . .

Susan (*simultaneously with both of them*) Don't listen to either of them.
    They're such liars both of them . . .

Andy (*quietening them*) All right, all right, all right! One at a time. First of
    all, who is he? Second, what's he doing?

Lucy He's mad, that's all . . .

Andy Sssh! Susie, what's he doing here?

Susan Well, he was just—passing through . . .

Tony How can he be just passing through? It's a ten-mile walk to the main
    gate . . .

Lucy He was saying sweet things to Mother. She said so herself.

Andy Susie, are they telling the truth? Why are you protecting him? Is it
    true?

Susan I—I can't answer.

Andy Then I'll ask him. (*Calling across to Bill*) Hey, you!

Susan You can't ask him. He won't hear you . . .

*She tails away as Bill turns, puzzled, and stares at them. The skies grow
noticeably darker as he does so*

Andy Yes, you. I'm talking to you. What are you doing here?

Bill Oh, hallo. Were you talking to me?

Susan (*with a wail, at this new turn of events*) Oh, my God . . . Now what's
    happening?

Andy Have you been threatening my wife?

Bill Me? Good Lord, no.

Tony Who are you? Who were you talking to?

Bill Me? I'm a stockbroker and whizz-kid wheeler-dealer and I was trying to remember a poem.

Lucy A likely story. Punch him, Daddy.

Susan No, Andy . . .

Bill (*alarmed*) Just a tick——

Tony (*advancing menacingly*) If there's one thing I loathe and detest it's stockbrokers. What have you got in that case?

Bill Nothing, nothing . . .

Susan Don't hurt him!

Lucy (*jumping up and down*) Rabbits. He's got rabbits in that case. Our rabbits.

Bill No, I haven't.

Tony Have you got some of our rabbits in your case?

Bill Of course not.

Lucy Yes, he has. I heard him talking to them.

Tony (*swooping and grabbing the case with great speed*) Let's take a look, then.

Bill Hey no, you can't have that. No . . .

Susan Stop it! Stop it!

Tony tosses the case to Lucy who catches it

Tony Have a look, Lucy.

Lucy starts to open the case. Bill hops about trying to retrieve it from her but Tony blocks his path. Susan moves forward to assist Bill but is restrained gently but firmly by Andy

Bill Look, you mustn't . . . You won't be able to open it anyway, it's jammed.

Lucy What have we in here . . . ?

Tony (*to Bill*) All right, take it easy. Take it easy.

Susan Bill . . . Andy, please——

Andy It's all right, Susie. Leave it to them.

Susan But they mustn't touch his case, it's——

Andy No, darling. He may be a poacher. If he's a poacher then we'll have to hang him.

Susan Hang him?

Bill What's that about hanging?

Lucy opens the case. It contains just one item. She drops the case and holds up a long garment which appears to have been made entirely of knotted string

Lucy (*with a cry of glee*) Look what I've found! It's a dress. It's a lovely macramé dress. Thank you very much.

Bill No, no. That's not for you. Put that back. That's my daughter's—for her school concert. Put it back, I say . . .

Lucy (*rushing off*) I can't wait to try it on . . .

Lucy goes off

Bill snatches up his discarded briefcase and follows her

Bill Please don't. Please be careful. It isn't finished. There's another six weeks' work . . .

Bill goes off after her

Tony makes to follow

Tony (*to Andy*) What do you want me to do with him?
Andy (*with a glance at Susan*) Oh, just chuck him in the lake for the time being.
Susan Oh, Bill ...
Andy (*after the departing Tony*) Gently, Tony. Do it gently.
Tony (*as he goes*) Righty-ho ...

Tony goes off

It is now sunset again, as in the earlier scene when Andy and Susan were alone together

Susan Oh, they're both so naughty.
Andy Don't be too hard on them, Susie.
Susan Tony you expect it from. But Lucy ...
Andy Well ... You have to make allowances for a girl. After all, the night before her wedding. She's bound to be a bit overexcited, isn't she?
Susan Yes, of course ...
Andy Remember our wedding day?
Susan What a question ...
Andy We must try and make Lucy's day just as wonderful.
Susan Nothing could ever be like ours. Remember our honeymoon? Remember Portugal?
Andy I do.
Susan And our first house? How poor we were, then.
Andy I had to sell my desk and my swivel chair, so we could eat ...

They laugh

Susan Eat? What about that first meal I cooked for us? In the pressure cooker?
Andy Best meal I've ever eaten off the ceiling.

They laugh again

Susan You've never let me live that down. Not after—what is it?—ten years.
Andy Eleven. You're still as young. You haven't changed. Just the same.
Susan Will Lucy's husband like me?
Andy He will adore you. She will be wild with jealousy, mark my words. (*Moving to her*) And if you reciprocate in the slightest way, so will I be.

He kisses her softly. They sink to the ground

Susan (*murmuring*) Oh, Andy ...

Andy kisses her again, fleetingly

Andy Shhh!

He gently lies her back on the grass. He starts to kiss her neck. As he does so, Susan opens her eyes in brief horror, suddenly aware of her predicament

Susan (*as he continues kissing her, softly*) Oh, dear God! I'm making love with the Devil ... (*She closes her eyes and surrenders to the happily inevitable*)

Simultaneously there is a Black-out, during which Andy exits

Then a tremendous clap of thunder. A short pause while it dies, then rain, a further rumble and a flash of lightning. Susan is revealed in the same place as before, on the grass, sprawled out, eyes now open, a smile on her face. Rain is pouring down on her. Andy has gone. The dress Susan was wearing before has been loosened, perhaps unbelted at the waist to suggest that she is now in a nightdress. She has also shed her shoes

Gerald (*off, distant*) Susan! Susan! Where are you?

Susan half-registers this, but doesn't move

In a moment, from the direction of the house, Gerald's torch is seen bobbing into view. When he appears, we see he is dressed in dressing-gown and slippers over his pyjamas

(*Appearing*) Susan! Where have you gone? Su——? (*He stops short as the torch beam falls upon Susan lying on the grass*) Susan? What on earth's happened to you? Susan?

Susan (*dreamily*) Mmmm?

Gerald (*calling back behind him*) It's all right, she's here. She's out here. Lying in the middle of the lawn. (*Returning to her*) Susan, can you hear me?

Susan Hallo, Gerald. How are things?

Gerald (*angrier now*) What on earth do you think you're playing at, woman? Lying out here on the grass at half-past three in the morning? In the middle of a thunderstorm? Is this some sort of a joke?

Susan Yes. Terribly funny, isn't it?

Gerald No, it is not funny, Susan. It is not funny at all. Now please get up and come indoors. Up! Up!

Susan Nope! Nope!

Gerald (*really angry*) Susan! Come along. (*He seizes one of her hands and attempts to pull her to her feet or even, possibly, along the ground*) Hup ... hup ... oh ... (*He gives up the struggle. It is more difficult than he thought. Rather breathless now*) Susan, I'm warning you, I shall——(*Turning and calling*) Rick! Rick! Come here! Give me a hand quickly, please! (*Returning to Susan again*) Susan, what has come over you? What on earth is the matter?

Susan I'm fine. Fine. You mustn't worry, Gerald, you really mustn't ...

Gerald (*calling*) Rick!

Susan We'll get a nice quiet divorce.

Gerald (*very startled*) Divorce?

Susan I promise I won't let it affect your career. I promise.

Gerald What?

Susan I won't make a scandal for you. I don't want to hurt you, really. I won't mention names, if you won't ...

Gerald (*furious*) What are you talking about? What on earth are you talking about? My dressing-gown is wringing wet, my bedroom slippers are full of rainwater and I haven't the faintest idea what you're talking about. (*Yelling*) Rick! Where the—blazes is that boy? Oh, yes. Well, if you want to know where he is, I'll tell you where he is. He's putting out the fire, that's where he is.

Susan Fire?

Gerald The fire that mercifully woke me up before we fried in our beds. The fire in my study, presumably started by you . . .

Susan Me? Never . . .

Gerald Don't try and deny it, Susan.

Susan I've been out here.

Gerald All sixty pages blazing away. Do you realize the years of work that went into that book? The research? The background reading? The hours of grubbing around, rubbing tombstones? I was on my final chapter, Susan. How could you do it? "And finally, what lessons are there to be learnt from the past six hundred years of parish history? For is it not the duty of the present to learn from the past in order to prepare for the——" Oh, God!

A clap of thunder

Forgive me for my feelings towards you at this moment, Susan. For they are unspeakable. Please come inside. I will forgive you in the dry.

Susan No, no. Don't worry about me. Go and look after your book, I'm all right . . .

Rick comes out from the house. He is dressed in similar fashion to Gerald. He holds one charred sheet of manuscript

Rick Sorry, Dad, I did my—— (*Seeing Susan*) Mum? What's the matter with Mum?

Gerald Did you manage to save any of it, Rick?

Rick What's the matter with Mum? What's she doing out here?

Gerald Never mind her. Did you manage to save any of my book?

Rick Well, yes. That. That's all.

Gerald (*snatching it from him and shining his torch on it*) Page fifty-seven (*Brandishing the page at Susan*) That's it. That's what's left. Are you satisfied, woman?

Susan It wasn't me——

Gerald (*dropping to his knees on the grass*) Why, Susan, why?

Susan —I've been out here.

Gerald Why? What terrible, nameless, unmentionable thing can I possibly have done to you?

Susan Married me?

Rick Look, don't you think you two had better come inside. It's pouring with rain. Hadn't you noticed?

Gerald Who cares, now? Who cares?

A slight pause. Just the sound of rain

(*Shrugging hopelessly*) Well . . .

From the house, Muriel's voice is heard emitting a terrible wail

(*Fearfully*) What, in the name of heaven, is that?

Another wail, slightly closer

Rick It's Auntie Muriel . . .

Gerald Well, what does she——? Oh no, you haven't been setting fire to her as well, have you? Please tell me you haven't.

Muriel comes staggering on, in her night attire and considerably distressed

Muriel He's back . . . Gerald, he's back. Harry's come back to me . . .

Rick Harry?

Gerald It's all right. It's just her husband.

Rick He's dead.

Muriel He's back. He's given me a sign, at last . . .

Gerald Oh, dear heaven, what a dreadful night. Forgive us, oh Lord, for all we have done to offend thee. Forgive us . . .

Muriel Oh, Gerald, but it's such a terrible sign. Oh, Harry . . .

Rick What's the problem, Auntie Muriel?

Muriel Rick, you'll have to come back in there with me. I can't go in there, not on my own . . . Not while he's there.

Rick Auntie, I can't. Look at Mum, she's——

Muriel lets out another wail

Gerald Go with her, Rick. It's nothing important. It happens to Muriel twice a week regularly. But for goodness' sake, go with her. Leave us. We'll manage somehow.

Rick (*starting to go*) Right. Are you sure? I won't be long . . .

Muriel Come on, quickly, Rickey, quickly . . .

Rick Coming, Auntie. (*To his parents as he goes*) Don't get too wet, will you?

Rick and Muriel go

Gerald and Susan continue to sit on the grass. The rain pours down

Gerald (*quietly*) Don't get too wet . . . Why did you do it, Susan? Do you hate me that much?

Susan I didn't do it. How many more times? But yes, as a matter of fact since you ask, I do hate you. Very much. But I didn't destroy your book, I promise. I think I know who did, though.

Gerald Who, if not you? Rick?

Susan No, not Ricky . . .

Gerald Well, who else is there? Muriel? A. J. P. Taylor, on a sudden jealous impulse? Who?

Susan Tony.

Gerald Tony? Tony who?

Susan My Tony. My brother Tony.

Gerald Don't be absurd. You have no brother. You did it. You know you did, admit it.

Susan No, I didn't. Because I was out here. All the time. And Bill Windsor can vouch for that. He came back and was with me. Till he was thrown in the lake. So.

Gerald Lake? What lake? Bill came back, yes, and you then felt dizzy and we had to put you to bed. And there you stayed, in bed asleep, from three p.m. onwards, until you awoke in the small hours and embarked on your nocturnal maraudings.

Susan That's nonsense. I know what I was doing and it certainly wasn't that——

Gerald Oh, yes, it was. There are witnesses.

Susan (*softly*) I'll never forget what I did. Ever.

Rick returns briefly with a dishcloth

Gerald Well?

Rick Very peculiar.

Gerald What is?

Rick She was right. Someone's written on her bedroom ceiling . . .

Gerald On Muriel's ceiling?

Rick In chalk, it looks like. They must have climbed on her chest of drawers . . .

Gerald Oh, Susan . . . What was written? Don't tell me.

Rick It says, "KNICKERS OFF, MURIEL".

Susan laughs

Gerald (*deeply shocked*) Oh, Susan. How is Muriel taking it?

Rick She's OK. I told her to make us all a cup of cocoa. Take her mind off it . . .

Gerald (*dully*) Cocoa?

Rick Won't be a minute. I'm going to clean it off for her.

Rick goes

Gerald All that and now compulsory cocoa. Locusts follow shortly. (*Rising and extending a hand*) Susan, come on inside, please.

Susan (*drawing back from him*) Go away, Gerald. Leave me alone.

Gerald Listen, I don't honestly have the energy left to drag you in by your hair. If you won't come of your own free will, then for your own sake, I shall be forced to phone an ambulance.

Susan Oh, not another ambulance . . .

Gerald You need to be looked after, Susan.

Susan I'm being looked after perfectly well, thank you. Now go away. (*Shouting*) Bugger off!

Gerald (*defeated*) I'm going! I'm going! I give up, Susan, I give up. You've won. I'm afraid I can't do any more. That's it. Finished.

Gerald leaves

Susan (*after him, as he goes*) I don't care. I'm free of you all now, you see. All of you. You with your prim little, frigid little, narrow-minded little meanness. And that priggish brat who's ashamed of me. Who'd faint at the sight of a pair of tits. As for her with her dead husband. No wonder he died. (*Yelling*) What are you hoping for, Muriel? A phantom pregnancy? (*She laughs*) Too late, dear. Too damn late. You and me both. Over the hill. Over the . . . (*She suddenly feels sorry for herself. She becomes more plaintive and tearful. She looks around her. In a small voice*) Where's everybody gone? They've all gone. (*She sings*) Rain, rain, go away . . . (*Calling softly*) Andy? (*She listens*) Lucy?

No reply

Tony? Remember me?

Silence

Oh.

A clap of thunder

Tony appears in the distance. He carries an unopened umbrella. He seems quite unaffected by the rain

Tony (*hailing her*) Susie!
Susan Tony?
Tony (*approaching*) Dear Big Sis. What are you doing now? You'll catch your deather.
Susan I know, I'm so silly. I got caught in the rain ...
Tony We really do have to keep an eye on you, don't we? You can't be trusted out on your own ...
Susan You'll just have to take care of me, Tony ...
Tony (*hugging her briefly*) We will. We will. (*Opening the umbrella*) Now, let's get you dry ...

The umbrella when opened is seen to be more of a sunshade or even a parasol, intended for sun rather than rain. Tony holds it over Susan's head. At once the weather is transformed. The rain stops. The sun shines and it is noon on a glorious country afternoon. The birds sing

There! Isn't that better?
Susan Oh, yes. (*She looks around her with pleasure*) Much, much better.

Tony, now we can see him more clearly, is wearing a smart country gentleman's suit with sporty waistcoat and a tweed cap. He seems dressed more for a day at the races than for a wedding. This impression is heightened by the steward's badge he is wearing on his lapel. Everything from here on is in a slightly heightened colour and design, suggesting Susan's own extreme mental state. What we see are images remembered by her from films she has seen, books she has read, TV she has watched

Tony Perfect day for it, isn't it?
Susan (*happily*) Oh, yes. A perfect day for a wedding. Everything's perfect now ...

Lucy comes rushing on excitedly. She is wearing a wedding dress but, as yet, no head-dress. She carries a number of "extras" for Susan who is still very much in her nightdress state. Simple things to effect a quick transformation. A hat, gloves, shoes and some dress trimmings. Lucy also helps Susan during the next

Lucy Oh, there you are, Mother. I wondered where you were ...
Susan Darling, you look beautiful ...
Lucy (*kissing her lightly on the cheek*) Thank you. And you are quite hopeless. You know that, don't you?
Susan (*with an amused glance to Tony*) Yes, darling ...
Lucy I thought that today you were all supposed to run around after me and not the other way round ...

Susan I'm sorry. I was dreadfully delayed. I had to supervize this new maid, Tess. Who's terribly slow and frightfully dim ...

Tony Don't worry. Lucy adores running around ...

Tony saunters off during the next

Lucy No, I don't, shut up. Oh, Mummy, I'm terribly excited. I really am. I hope I'm going to be all right. That I won't let you and Daddy down.

Susan You won't, darling. Don't worry. We'll both be here.

Lucy (*whispering*) You'll be there tonight if I need you, won't you?

Susan I'll be there tonight if you need me, I promise.

Susan is putting on her shoes. While she does so, Lucy surveys the scene

Lucy Isn't that main marquee just sensational? It must cover about three acres. And it's simply filled with flowers.

Susan They're for you, darling. I got them all for you.

Andy strolls on. He is wearing morning dress and a grey top hat. He has a pair of binoculars round his neck

Andy Hallo, young Lucy.

Lucy (*running to kiss him*) Daddy, it's all perfect. Thank you. Thank you.

Andy We're doing our best. (*To Susan*) All right, darling?

Susan Very happy. (*She mouths "Thank you" to him*)

Andy (*throwing a kiss to Susan: to Lucy*) Incidentally, young lady, aren't you supposed to be ready for the off in a few minutes!

Lucy (*unconcernedly*) Plenty of time.

Andy Oh, yes? (*Producing a pocket watch and holding it up for her to see*) What does that say, then?

Lucy Oh, gosh. Golly, is that really the time? Do excuse me, everyone. Sorry ...

Lucy races off. Susan and Andy watch her with affectionate amusement

Susan I've never seen her so excited. Thank you for making it so perfect for her, Andy. You're being terribly patient. You know what these things mean to us women.

Andy If it makes you both happy, then I'm happy. I think everything's arrived anyway. Except the band. Where on earth has the band got to?

Exactly on cue a brass band strikes up in the distance with some cheerful tune

That's more like it.

Susan Oh, they're rather jolly ...

Andy Are you sure? We've got a pipe band if you'd rather.

The pipe band plays briefly

Susan No, these are fine.

The other band resumes

Tony strolls back into view

Andy All OK, Tony?

Tony You bet. I've just been having a snoop round the brides' enclosure.

Our Lucy looks as good as any of them, I must say ...
Susan (*rather puzzled*) Sorry?
Andy Glad to hear it.
Tony I think she'll do it, you know. She's in peak condition, she's free of injuries and, of course, the going'll suit her.
Andy She prefers it firm ...
Tony Oh, yes.
Susan What are you both talking about?

From the distance, over the band, the sound of the P.A. It is hard to make out distinctly, but it seems to be announcing a list of runners for the next race

Andy (*hearing this*) Hallo. Things are getting started.
Susan Will someone tell me what's going on?
Tony Aha! Look who's here ...

Bill enters. He is dressed in a rather loud, cliché bookie's suit. He still clutches his case as always. Only this one is emblazoned with the words "HONEST BILL"

Bill Afternoon, chaps.
Susan (*uncomprehendingly*) Bill?
Bill Hallo, Susie.
Andy How's the betting been?
Bill Oh, pretty brisk ...
Susan I thought this was a wedding.
Andy Put a tenner on for me, will you, Bill?
Bill Will do. Each way?
Susan Andy, I thought this was a wedding ...
Andy (*amused*) What's that about a wedding, you daft old thing? (*Ignoring her again*) What are you offering, Bill? Ten to one?
Tony You'll be lucky.
Bill No way, five to four and that's generous. You won't get that anywhere else ...
Andy What? She was thirty-three to one this morning ...
Bill No, that was the jockey. You can have thirty-three on him. Only five to four on the bride ...

The three men laugh uproariously at this. Susan watches them incredulously

Susan Aren't they getting married?
Bill Married? Who's getting married?
Andy Susie's got this thing about a wedding. She wants a wedding, for some reason ...
Tony Then you shall have a wedding, my darling ...
Susan I thought this was one ...
Bill Absolutely. Good things, weddings.
Andy (*his binoculars raised*) I think they're coming under orders ...
Susan (*becoming increasingly concerned*) Andy? Andy?
Andy (*absorbed*) Just a tick, darling ...
Bill (*chattily, to Tony*) Glorious spot, this. Is it all yours?
Tony Yes.
Bill How long have you lived here?

Tony Since thirteen eighty-six.
Bill Oh, quite a time. Vast.
Tony Yes, we go right to the river that way.
Bill Oh, yes. I see. What's the other side, then?
Tony Oh, that's Thailand ...
Bill Oh, is it? Is it?
Tony We held on to the shooting rights, but it's theirs officially.
Bill Lucky little chaps ...
Susan (*becoming impatient with this talk*) Oh, really. Do be sensible.
Bill And the lake there?
Tony No, that's the Caspian Sea.
Bill Is it? Is it? I always wondered where that was.
Susan Look, will you stop it at once, you two. You're spoiling it all.
Andy (*still with the glasses*) Ah! They're off ...
Bill Splendid!
Tony Hoorah!
Susan Where's my wedding? What's happened to the wedding I was promised? I want a wedding ...
Andy Hold on, darling, hold on. There's a love. (*At the race*) Good girl ... look at her go!
Tony Time for a glass of champers, I think, don't you?
Bill Rather.
Tony (*yelling to someone in the far distance*) Champagne over here ... Quick, quick ...
Andy She's lying third at the moment. But she's nicely positioned. Not letting herself get boxed in ...
Susan (*desperately to herself*) This isn't what I wanted at all. Not at all.

Muriel comes across the lawn with a tray of champagne glasses. She is dressed in very formal maid's black bombazine, with cap and apron. Incongruously, she appears to be heavily pregnant

Muriel Here comes a lovely glass of champagne ...
Tony Thank you, Muriel.
Susan (*recognizing her*) Muriel?
Muriel Just one moment, madam.
Bill (*taking a glass of champagne*) Super. Just what the doc ordered.

Tony also helps himself. Muriel does a lot of curtsying

First-rate band this. Who are they?
Tony Oh, they're all—hang on—who are they, Andy?
Andy (*still watching the race*) Odd-job men ...
Tony That's it. They're all odd-job men. Cornish odd-job men.
Bill Amazing.
Muriel (*offering Susan a glass*) Madam?
Susan This is all getting so stupid ...
Andy She's going to win it, you know, she's going to win!

Susan reacts to something in her drink

Susan Yeeurrk! This is disgusting. What's this in my drink?
Muriel In the champagne, madam?

Susan It's disgusting, take it away.

Muriel I think it's supposed to be there, madam. It was in the red tin.

Tony It's only a frog, Susie.

Susan A frog?

Tony If you don't like it, spit it out . . .

Susan (*sharply*) Muriel, get out of that ridiculous uniform, you look absurd . . .

Muriel Yes, madam. (*Curtsying*) Thank you, madam.

Tony Get 'em off, Muriel.

Muriel goes

Andy They've got about a furlong to go . . . It's Lucy from Macramé Lad and Dead Hubby . . . and they're well clear of Priggish Boy and Smug Vicar . . .

Susan (*impatiently*) Andy . . .

Andy Sorry, darling. Want a look?

Susan No, I don't. I've no desire to see our daughter prancing about singing dreadful songs in woolly animal ears.

Andy Oh, come on, darling. It's only once a year. And it means so much to the kid. (*Back to his binoculars*) And she's there . . . she's nearly there . . . and she's done it! Lucy's done it!

Tony Well done, Lucy . . .

Bill (*with him*) Good for her. First rate. In my opinion as a doctor, your maid's pregnant again, Andy. I could be wrong, of course.

Andy 'Fraid she is, Bill. Every time there's a race meeting, same old story . . . Excuse me, I'm just going to congratulate Lucy . . . Terrific race. (*He starts to move off*)

Susan (*vainly, after him*) Andy, wait . . .

At this moment Gerald enters. He is dressed as an Archbishop

Andy (*greeting him like a long-lost brother*) Hey! Hey! Look who's better late than never. Gerry! By all that's holy!

Gerald (*embracing Andy with equal fervour*) Andy, you old devil you . . .

Susan (*absolutely appalled*) Gerald?

Tony Hallo, Gerry!

Susan What's Gerald doing here?

Gerald Tony, you old rascal . . . And there's Billy Beelzebub himself. Hallo, Bill.

Bill Hallo, Gerry . . .

Gerald Well, this is nice, isn't it? Isn't this nice?

Susan Gerald, just go away. Go on, get away! Get away!

She is ignored. In fact, from this point on, people appear to be less and less aware of Susan. As if she herself were slowly slipping from the dream whilst it carries on without her

Andy Where have you been, anyway?

Gerald I do apologize, everyone. I had a divorce to perform. Last-minute job.

Bill Oh, super. I love divorces.

Andy Now, you must come and meet Lucy . . .

But at this moment, Lucy comes rushing on breathlessly, her face flushed with excitement. She is dressed as before, but now wears her head-dress. This is a standard bridal one, enlivened by the addition of a pair of built-in animal ears and a race winner's rosette. Behind her, she drags Rick. He is dressed as a sort of rickshaw driver—at least, as seen in various Hollywood oriental films

Lucy Daddy, we won. We won ...

Andy I know, darling, I know ...

Susan (*looking at the couple in horror*) No! Not Him. Not him, Lucy darling, don't marry him ... (*Shouting at Rick*) Go away, go away at once, Ricky! You're not to marry her, I forbid it.

Lucy It's no good, Mother, he doesn't speak English.

Tony They've been married for months, anyway.

Andy Never mind. I know you'll make Tess a fine husband, young man.

Susan Tess?

Rick (*in his normal voice*) I'll try sir. I'll do my best to fatten her up and cut off her hair.

Gerald God bless you, God bless you, God bless you ...

At this point, everyone, with the exception of Susan, now totally ignored, gathers round the bride and groom and talks at once. Susan watches them with increasing fury

Lucy I knew I was going to win. I looked round during those final three furlongs and I could see the other two were getting weaker. And I felt as strong as ever. I could have run and run all day long ... *etc.*

Rick (*with her*) I knew we were in with a chance. But it was Tess, she was the one. She showed her convent training. I've never been so proud in my life. Don't worry, I'll take good care of her, you can be sure of that ... *etc.*

Andy (*with them*) I had the glasses on you all the way. I was a bit concerned at the five furlong marker when you still hadn't made a break but I understood your tactics. I mean, the thing about having a fast finish is to use it, isn't it? ... *etc.*

Tony (*with them*) I think the wonderful thing about racing is that it doesn't matter a damn about the races. The whole thing's one glorious social event, in my opinion, intended for the consumption of the maximum number of bottles of champers ... *etc.*

Bill (*with them*) This is the most glorious race course I've ever been on. I think it beats somewhere like Ascot into a top hat. I mean, you've got everything. Thailand over there and the Caspian. And the best of England as well. Magic ... *etc.*

Gerald (*with them*) You know I haven't been here since—when would it be?—thirteen eighty-six, I think. Can it be that long? You don't look a day older, Andy, old boy. I hope the same can be said about me. I doubt it. Some of us wear better then others, eh? ... *etc.*

Susan (*after a moment of this*) This is grossly unfair, it really is. Why doesn't anyone take any notice of me? (*Louder*) Why won't you look at me? (*Very loudly*) LOOK AT ME AT ONCE, DO YOU HEAR? ALL OF YOU!!! (*She stamps her foot*)

The band stops playing. Silence. Everyone turns to look at her. They seem slightly puzzled for a moment as to who she might be

Andy (*moving forward, as he remembers her*) Darling ...
Lucy Mother, how lovely ...

They all surge forward to greet her. Susan is a little alarmed

Susan What are you all doing?

They surround her, greeting her as they do so. All seem pleased to see her

Muriel comes on unobtrusively with more champagne. She is no longer pregnant

Rick (*again, together with the others*) Hallo there, Mum. Good to see you ...
Gerald (*with him*) Hallo, Susan. Do you remember me? Gerald?
Bill (*with them*) Hallo, there. Are you still taking those pills I gave you?
Tony (*with them*) Hallo, Big Sis. Where have you been hiding away?
Andy (*over this*) Ladies and Gentlemen ... I have ... Ladies and Gentlemen ...

The chatter dies down

(*Seeing*) Have we got some fresh champagne there, Muriel? Splendid. Pass it round.
Muriel Yes, sir. (*Confidentially, with a furtive look in Susan's direction*) The ambulance is on its way ...
All (*except Susan, furtively to Muriel*) Shhh!

There is a single clap of thunder. One or two react but the weather remains unalterably sunny. Muriel passes amongst them. Those with no glasses take one. Those with empty ones take full ones. Susan is not offered one and seems, during the course of things, to have lost her original glass

Andy (*as Muriel performs her duties*) You've had the baby all right, I see, Muriel?
Muriel Yes, sir. Thank you, sir.
Andy What was it? Another boy?
Muriel Yes, sir.
Andy And what are you going to call him? Let me guess?
Muriel Harry, sir.
Andy Splendid. That'll be—how many—now?
Muriel This'll be my tenth Harry, sir.
Andy Well done. Keep going.

A small ripple of applause. Muriel looks embarrassed

(*Seeing they are all set*) Now then. Muriel, grab yourself a glass, you must join us for this ...

Muriel does so, standing just a little apart from the circle

Ladies and Gentlemen, I want to propose a toast to the woman who is not simply the most important person in my life—but I suspect, is the most important person in all our lives ...

All (*variously*) Hear . . . hear . . . absolutely . . . *etc.*

Andy Susan, you are uniquely precious to us all. You are irreplaceable.

Susan glows

So, without further frills. To you, dearest Susie.

All (*toasting*) Dearest Susie. (*They drink*)

Tony Speech . . .

Lucy Yes, speech, Mummy . . .

Susan (*deferentially*) No, no . . .

All (*variously*) Yes, yes . . . speech . . . come on, Susie, speech . . .

Susan, still standing amongst them, smiles in acceptance. She bows her head slightly in thought and then starts her speech. The others step back so that she stands in a larger circle than before

Susan Dearest friends. Family. My happiest moment has been to stand here with you all and share this, my most precious of days. I grow hugh, summer few bald teddy know these two wonderful children, Lucy and Rick. I cannot tell you how heaply cowed siam.

As she continues to speak the Lights begin to fade round her until finally she is isolated

Tinny beers a show. High december how rotten high trade fat haywood throw twig and throng hike hair share rents. Pie lank hod hat day lid! Hens, hang few saw paw up-short. Hang few. Hang few, hens, sizzle pie tart insole. Grey ice way chew . . . ? (*She hesitates*) Grey ice way . . . ?

She is aware that people seem to be getting harder to see. She is starting to be lit now by the reflection of an ambulance's blue flashing light

Hair growing, hens? Goosey? Gandy? Chair old? (*She pauses*) Hair shone? Hair hall shone? Tone show, fleas, Fleas, tone show. December bee? Choose 'un. December choosey. December bee? December bee?

The others have frozen in the shadows. They appear neither to see nor to hear her now. Susan gives a last despairing wail. As she does so, the Lights fade to Black-out

CURTAIN

FURNITURE AND PROPERTY LIST

ACT I

On stage: Grass
Trees
Shrubs
Flowers
Rockery
Small pond. *By it:* stone frog
Dustbins
Rake
Medical case for **Bill**
Upstage (behind gauze): 6 trees (*Note:* in the London production, the upstage "dream" part of the garden changed each time Susan's imaginary family appeared—topiary arches (page 17), rose arch (page 19), swing and statue (page 27)

Off stage: Tennis racket **(Lucy)**
Tennis racket, glass of champagne **(Tony)**

During black-out on page 10:

Strike: Rake

Set: 3 garden chairs

Off stage: Tray with 3 cups of coffee **(Muriel)**
2 glasses of champagne **(Lucy)**
Glass of champagne **(Lucy)**
Tray with dusty bottle of Marsala, assorted glasses; folding card table **(Gerald)**
Bowl of nuts **(Muriel)**
Garden table with 4 place settings **(Tony)**
2 chairs **(Lucy)**
2 chairs **(Tony)**
3 champagne glasses, bottle of champagne **(Lucy)**
Serving platter of elaborately garnished cold salmon **(Andy)**

Personal: **Susan:** wedding ring (required throughout)
Bill: wrist-watch (required throughout)
Gerald: spectacles (required throughout)

ACT II

Strike: Garden table and place settings, salmon, champagne, glasses

Set: *Upstage (behind gauze):* hedge, high swing (*Note:* Upstage garden changes in Act II were as follows—hedges, statues and sundial (page 45), everything upstage of gauze struck completely (page 54)

Off stage: Shotgun (broken open), game bag **(Tony)**
Tray with 4 cups of coffee **(Muriel)**
Shotgun, bloodstained game bag **(Tony)**
Medical case containing macramé dress **(Bill)**
Torch—practical, on **(Gerald)**
Charred sheet of manuscript **(Rick)**
Dishcloth **(Rick)**
Umbrella/parasol **(Tony)**
Hat, gloves, shoes, dress trimmings for Susan **(Lucy)**
Medical case with "Honest Bill" on each side **(Bill)**
Tray with glasses of champagne, each containing a small toy frog, pregnancy padding **(Muriel)**
Bishop's crook **(Gerald)**
Tray with glasses of champagne **(Muriel)**

Personal: **Bill:** bottle of pills, handkerchief in pocket
Tony: steward's badge
Andy: binoculars round neck, pocket watch
Lucy: bridal head-dress with animal ears and winner's rosette

LIGHTING PLOT

Property fittings required: nil

Exterior. A garden. The same scene throughout

ACT I

To open: Black-out

Cue 1	**As Susan** moans *Gradually bring up bright sunshine downstage*	(Page 1)
Cue 2	**Susan** (*to herself, puzzled*): "Dog? I can't hear a dog ..." *Increase lighting, bringing up dreamlike lighting upstage (6 trees)*	(Page 3)
Cue 3	**Andy** exits *Fade lighting upstage, return to previous lighting downstage*	(Page 6)
Cue 4	**Susan**'s knees buckle, she gives a terrible moan and falls into a faint *Black-out*	(Page 10)
Cue 5	When ready, as **Susan** jolts awake with a cry *Bring up bright morning sunshine downstage*	(Page 10)
Cue 6	**Gerald:** "When I write. Well." *Briefly bring up dreamlike lighting upstage (topiary arches)— fade as **Tony** chases **Lucy** off*	(Page 17)
Cue 7	**Lucy** enters with 2 glasses of champagne *Bring up dreamlike lighting upstage (rose arch)*	(Page 19)
Cue 8	**Lucy** goes, taking **Susan**'s glass *Fade lighting upstage*	(Page 20)
Cue 9	**Gerald** goes, **Susan** hesitates then reluctantly makes to follow *Bring up dreamlike lighting upstage (swing and statue)*	(Page 27)
Cue 10	**Susan** sinks into a drink-induced oblivion *Black-out*	(Page 30)

ACT II

To open: Black-out

Cue 11	**As Susan** groans *Gradually bring up sunshine downstage*	(Page 31)
Cue 12	**Susan:** "Well, what did you expect?" *Bring up dreamlike lighting upstage (high swing and hedge)*	(Page 32)
Cue 13	**Lucy** rises and rushes away *Fade lighting upstage*	(Page 37)

Cue 14	**Susan** stares at the sky and listens *Decrease lighting, as though moving towards sunset, upstage also*	(Page 38)
Cue 15	**Andy** goes *Fade upstage lighting, return to normal mild afternoon light downstage*	(Page 41)
Cue 16	As **Lucy** wanders on *Bring up dreamlike lighting upstage (hedge, statues and sundial)*	(Page 45)
Cue 17	As **Bill** turns, puzzled, and stares at them *Skies grow noticeably darker*	(Page 47)
Cue 18	**Tony** goes off *Sunset lighting*	(Page 49)
Cue 19	**Susan:** "I'm making love with the Devil ..." (*She closes her eyes*) *Black-out*	(Page 50)
Cue 20	As tremendous clap of thunder dies *Rain effect, then flash of lightning; bring up night lighting downstage*	(Page 50)
Cue 21	**Tony** holds parasol over **Susan**'s head *Cut rain effect; bring up glorious afternoon sunshine—blue sky upstage*	(Page 54)
Cue 22	**Andy:** "Ah! They're off ..." *Sky gradually turns from blue to red*	(Page 57)
Cue 23	**Susan:** "... heaply cowed siam ..." *Begin to fade lights to spot on* **Susan**	(Page 61)
Cue 24	**Susan:** "Grey ice way ..." *Reflection of ambulance's flashing light*	(Page 61)
Cue 25	As **Susan** gives a last despairing wail *Fade to black-out*	(Page 61)

EFFECTS PLOT

ACT I

Cue 1   As **Bill** enters   (Page 6)
Dog howls briefly in distance

Cue 2   **Bill:** "Ah, yes. Silly question."   (Page 8)
Dog howls in distance—continue for a few minutes

Cue 3   **Susan:** "... won't even speak to me——"   (Page 17)
Pause, then dog starts howling in distance—fade after a few moments

ACT II

Cue 4   Black-out   (Page 50)
Tremendous clap of thunder; pause, then rain effect, further rumble of thunder—continue rain

Cue 5   **Gerald:** "Oh, God!"   (Page 51)
Clap of thunder

Cue 6   **Susan:** "Remember me?" (*Silence*) "Oh."   (Page 54)
Clap of thunder

Cue 7   **Tony** holds parasol over **Susan**'s head   (Page 54)
Cut rain effect; bring up birdsong

Cue 8   **Andy:** "... has the band got to?"   (Page 55)
Brass band strikes up in distance

Cue 9   **Andy:** "... got a pipe band if you'd rather."   (Page 55)
Pipe band replaces brass band

Cue 10   **Susan:** "No, these are fine."   (Page 55)
Brass band resumes

Cue 11   **Susan:** "... both talking about?"   (Page 56)
Indistinct PA in distance, over sound of band, announcing list of runners

Cue 12   **Susan:** "ALL OF YOU!!!" (*She stamps her foot*)   (Page 60)
Cut brass band

Cue 13   **All** (*except Susan, furtively to Muriel*): "Shhh!"   (Page 60)
Single clap of thunder

MADE AND PRINTED IN GREAT BRITAIN BY
LATIMER TREND & COMPANY LTD PLYMOUTH
MADE IN ENGLAND